Mrs Beeton's Best Bits

A guide to her tragic history and her social and culinary insights

Wtih her 40 best recipes

David Cohen

Published by Psychology News Press

psychologynews@hotmail.com

Distributed by Melia Publishing Services

melia@melia.org

Telephone: 01483 869 839

British Library Cataloguing in Publication Data

A catalogue record for this book is available from the British Library

ISBN 0-9076-3321-8
ISBN 13 978-0-907633-21-1

Designed by Paul Lawrence

Cartoons by Daniel McConnell

Printed and bound in Great Britain by Biddles, Kings Lynn, Norfolk

Borrowed Items 01/02/2010

XXXX2157

Item Title	Due Date
Modern cookery for private f:	22/02/2010
Sichuan cookery	22/02/2010
Mrs Beeton's best bits : a gu	22/02/2010

Contents

When historians look at today's culture where a thousand cook books and TV shows bloom, it won't just be the recipes that interest them. The Germans put it well – "man ist wass Mann ist" – you are what you eat. But it is not just what you eat that makes you. How, when and with whom you share food also says something about you. "Sausage and chips most days of the week" bloke is likely to be a little different from tomatoes provencale drizzled with extra virgin oil man.

peak foods

Delve into Delia Smith, journey round Jamie Oliver, research Ramsay and you'll learn much about the way we live now – our fears, our snobberies, our hopes. We are in a foodie culture. We worry about how food will affect us. A good diet can keep you slim, stave off cancer, boost your chances of still being sexy at sixty six. Will you still need me, will you still feed me when I'm 64 is old hat since 60 is the new 40.

Food has become what the psychologist Abraham Maslow called one of our "peak experiences". The Guardian discussed on March 24 2006 the question of whether there could be intellectual property rights in recipes.

We are also becoming ever more baroque in our search for the perfect meal and the perfect restaurant. Thousands of words are devoted every day to finding the best restaurant in the universe. Restaurants are rated on their food, their service, their décor and their avant garde wow factor. Isabella Beeton never doubted cooking was an art but, for her, it was essentially a conventional art. Recipes did not get extra marks because they were the best of "experimental art" cooking.

We, however, are constantly searching for the new and the more perfect – the Picasso of pasta. Nothing else explains the current fashion for ice cream made out of stuff that has never been ice-creamed before, like bacon and eggs ice cream which, darlings, you simply must taste.

Followed by a baked bean reduction!

Guzzling books

And if you can't eat it, read it. We devour books about food. According to Amazon's web sites, there are 190 books on olive oil only, tasty tomes which draw subtle distinctions between Lucca oil, Lesbos oil and olive oil which has been hand pressed by virgins on their luscious thighs. I particularly like Passionate Olive Oil. I didn't make that up – any more than I made up bacon and eggs ice cream.

None of this would have surprised Isabella Beeton. She knew there was more to eating than food. She pointed out;

"Man is the only animal who dines. Other species eat. But only man dines."

Boar's head for dinner

That epigram introduced 75 pages in her book of menus for all kinds of dinner parties. Some occasions merited a mere 4 courses, more formal dinners needed 6 courses, and the super formal probably needed more than 8 crowned with a "Grim boar's head" dressed with rosemary. Isabella also devised ideal menus for every single month of the year, using foods that were "seasonable," one of her favourite words.

Later editions of the book produced dinner party menus in both French and English

Chez Bruce

Potage a la bonne femme

Petits Pates de homard

Selle d'Agneau, Sauce
Menthe

Gelinotte de bois roti

Salade

Pouding au marrrons

Crème au cafe

Aigrettes au Parmesan

Chez Beeton

Good Wife Soup

Lobster Patties

Saddle of Lamb with mint
sauce

roast Hazel Hen

Salad

Chestnut Pouding

Coffee Cream

Parmesan fritters

Followed by fruit, port, liqueur, cigars.

If you wish to give your G.P a heart attack, tell him that is what you intend to eat soon!

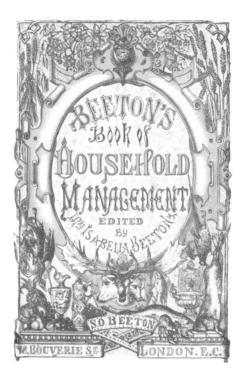

The history of Isabella

Isabella Beeton was a pioneer, the first person to write a very practical
book on how to cook from A to Y, from Almonds to Yorkshire Pudding.
She doesn't seem to have any entries under Z. But she covered more than
kitchen matters. She also offered advice on how to run a house, rear your
babies, deal with doctors and how to cope in an emergency. Accidents are,
alphabetically, the first entry in her "Analytical Index." She even wrote over
2000 words on how to bleed one of your relatives if his or her life were at
risk and you could not find a doctor fast.

The Victorian mistress of the house could face so many crises. Isabella
told her readers what they had to do to produce the perfect dinner party,
how to cope with teething, deal with constipation, keep the staff in check,
bring up the children, deal with the domestics, check that the housekeeper
was not nicking the housekeeping budget – and much else beside. Mrs
Conscientious 1861 didn't need to buy another book to turn herself into
the model housewife who would please her husband. Isabella drew the line,
however, at giving advice on what to do in bed.

Artichokes and the Bible

I had never read Mrs Beeton till the spring 2005. Then, I picked up a copy of The Book of General Household Management which belonged to a friend of mine, Paul Lawrence. I was avoiding making phone calls; I was not remotely looking for a recipe. But, as I turned the pages, I was hooked.

It wasn't the recipes that hooked me so much as Isabella's footnotes and her many asides. They are learned, witty and, sometimes, even a bit intense. She included a huge range of references from Greek mythology to contemporary poems. She liked verse and often included poems about sheep, boar's heads, hermit crabs, lobsters and salads.

All right, sheep have often been the subject of verse. But lettuce? An Ode to lettuce?

Her asides often make Isabella seem like an eager student out to impress her teachers. That reflects something we have forgotten. The woman who wrote this magisterial cookbook was not a matron in her 50s who had seen everything in the home and kitchen, but a young woman of 24. And that young woman was, as all good compilers are, endlessly curious. Why else would she tell us about such topics as;

The role the artichoke played in the Bible.

The best time to kill a calf if you want to get really tasty veal cutlet.

The number of oysters which were sold on the London fish market in 1860 – just a few short of 5000 million.

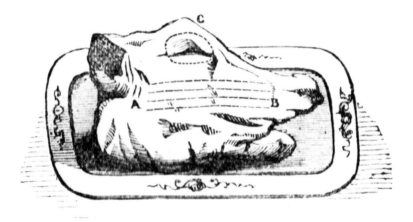

help! i'm choking!

Mrs Freud and Mrs Beeton

She was also very determined to make one patriotic point. There was much to admire about French cuisine but that was no reason to accept all the extravagant claims the French made about how to cook. It was not as if other nations did not have cuisines of their own.

Isabella had her passions. She was poetic about the mackerel - and intense about the cabbage. Not because of its taste, but because of its medicinal properties. Cabbage could cure most human ills, she believed. The potato she didn't feel the same about.

When you read Isabella, you also get a wonderful feeling for the way in which Victorians lived. We think of them as industrial heroes who built roads, railways and other engineering marvels. They made the British Empire run and hum.

Well ho hum

As Freud (whose wife Martha used Beeton but complained she did not know how to make a strudel) explained stress causes psychosomatic problems. In The Interpretation of Dreams, Freud writes of food symbolism and tells the tale of a lawyer who bought two pears. His mother gave him one to eat but the second pear he was forbidden to touch. The pears were, of course, his mother's breasts.

I have scoured Freud for a mention of melons without any luck.

When you read Isabella you quickly realize how many of Victorians saw themselves as invalids. They then took, neurotically – and enthusiastically - to their beds and never budged. They had mind trouble and stomach trouble. Digestion was a big issue. Many vegetables just put too much strain on the delicate 19th century stomachs. But help was at hand.

Pigeon pie

Today only those who know their onions realize that Isabella Beeton was a tragic heroine who died younger than Emily Bronte and many of those 19th century romantic figures.

Isabella was born in 1836 in Cheapside. Her father died when she was only six leaving 3 other children. Then, Isabella's mother re-married and she had more children. Her second husband had a family by his first wife and Isabella grew up in a household with 20 children. Even by Victorian standards, a family with so many children was pushing it.

It was not just sheer numbers that made Isabella's family unusual. Her mother's second husband was the Clerk to the Racecourse at Epsom. With his job, he got accommodation – a set of rooms under the grandstand. Isabella never forgot where she lived because one of her recipes is called Epsom Grandstand pigeon pie. The Beeton children used the racecourse as their playground.

Isabella went to school in the City of London and then studied in Germany at Heidelberg. As a result, she spoke French and German and she was able to use a number of French books in her research. She admired some French cooking but had few good things to say about German cooking. After finishing her studies she returned to London and fell in love. She fell in love passionately as well as smartly, intelligently and creatively. Her love was Samuel Beeton,

Samuel was a successful publisher who had started to work in Fleet Street in his teens. He realized that, as more and more people could read, they wanted something other than the Bible. He started many 'penny dreadfuls' which offered readers sensation and information. By his late 20s, he was a mogul of popular magazines.

For an early press baron, Samuel was enlightened. He did not want to lock his wife up in the kitchen and nursery. An intelligent wife was "one of the greatest boons heaven has bestowed on man", he wrote. And Isabella was very intelligent. She threw herself with enthusiasm into her husband's business and made it even more successful.

As soon as she married Isabella spotted what modern marketing experts would call a gap in the market.

I really havn't a clue what to do with the butler!

There were no books available for the young woman who suddenly had to manage a large household. Growing up in a large family influenced her view of how a kitchen and a household had to be managed.

The pen not the pan

Isabella often compared running a house to running a military operation. That's not surprising, as there were over 20 to sit down at dinner every night when she was a child.

As soon as she married, she started to write for Samuel's *Englishwoman's Domestic Magazine* and her masterpiece, The *Book of Household Management* grew out of her articles for that.

Isabella could be said to have been the first superwoman who juggled career, home and children.

The *Book of Household Management* was published in 1861 when Isabella was 25. The recipes were not the innovation. What was so new was that the book was so well organized and so comprehensive. The Victorian mistress did not have time to waste. So Isabella set out 2000 recipes in a format which became the standard for cookbooks ever after. She listed the ingredients, how to prepare them, how to cook them, and what it all cost.

Isabella never claimed to be a great cook. Her skill was with the pen, not the pan. Critics have accused her of using other people's recipes but that doesn't seem very fair. She often admits that a recipe comes from Soyer, a great French chef who wrote a *History of Food*, or Brillat Savarin, a lawyer who coped with the terrors of the French revolution by writing about food, or from other eminences.

Only one recipe is marked the "Authoress's recipe." It is for Baroness Pudding. Even then, far from pretending it is her own precious recipe, Isabella admits a friend of hers, who was indeed a baroness, gave her the details. The Baroness was a boiling enthusiast and insisted that the secret which made the pudding so wonderful was it was boiled and boiled and boiled over again. Isabella can't be accused of passing off other people's recipes as her own.

Isabella's great achievement was to research, collect, test, collate and standardize every recipe. Her book also aimed to be compendium of everything there was to know about food, how farms produced it, chemistry and cooking methods. Isabella was not sure, for example, that the new fangled gas cookers were either safe or economical.

new! fangled! gas stove

Charles Dickens and Arthur Conan Doyle speak

"A simple gas burner will consume more oxygen and produce more carbonic acid to deteriorate the atmosphere of a room than six candles." Was Isabella an early critic of carbon emissions?

Isabella managed to master the massive amount of detail and make her book interesting and accessible. It sold 60,000 copies in its first year – and has kept on selling. Dickens quoted it. Conan Doyle thought it was one of the great Victorian works.

Isabella often quoted French writers like the lawyer Brillat Savarin. But, apart from the French, she was not inclined to think other 'cuisines' had much to teach the Brits. Even though she lived in Heidelberg, she mentions few German recipes. There are a number of Italian dishes but, in general, her book celebrates British cooking with many Parisian frills. Some cultures were almost anti-food, she pointed out.

"The modern Egyptians are, in general, extremely temperate in regard to food. Even the richest among them take little pride, and perhaps, experience as little delight, in the luxuries of the table. Their dishes mostly consist of pilaus, soups, and stews, prepared principally of onions, cucumbers, and other cold vegetables, mixed with a little meat cut into small pieces. On special occasions, however, a whole sheep is placed on the festive board; but during several of the hottest months of the year, the richest restrict themselves entirely to a vegetable diet. The poor are contented with a little oil or sour milk, in which they may dip their bread."

The writing and research of the book cost Isabella a great deal. Her first sentences of the preface read;

———◦◦———

> I MUST frankly own, that if I had known, beforehand, that this book would have cost me the labour which it has, I should never have been courageous enough to commence it. What moved me, in the first instance, to attempt a work like this, was the discomfort and suffering which I had seen brought upon men and women by household mismanagement. I have always thought that there is no more fruitful source of family discontent than a housewife's badly-cooked dinners and untidy ways. Men are now so well served out of doors,—at their clubs, well-ordered taverns, and dining-houses, that in order to compete with the attractions of these places, a mistress must be thoroughly acquainted with the theory and practice of cookery, as well as be perfectly conversant with all the other arts of making and keeping a comfortable home.

She was not exaggerating. While she was writing the book, she lost her first two sons in infancy. Her third child lived. But then she became pregnant again. It seemed to be going well but then she got an infection and she died. In her text Isabella insists on the need for cleanliness but the midwife and attendants who were present when her fourth son was born did not clean themselves or their instruments properly. Isabella never recovered from the infection. The romantic novelist Emily Bronte made to it thirty before she died, living longer than Isabella. But we think of Bronte as a fragile artist and of Isabella as the sturdy kitchen mistress.

**Samuel Orchart Beeton
(ca. 1831-1877)**

Inner city asparagus

Many of Isabella's footnotes reveal much about the differences between the then – and now – of everyday life. There was no fast food. She says nothing about pizzas or, perhaps more surprising, charcuterie. I can find no entry for salami though there is a dish called Salmi of hashed partridge.

You would not expect Isabella to mention sushi, but there is no mention of any Chinese dish, even though both Victorian London and Liverpool had Chinese communities. Curries do occasionally get in, but the only mention of garlic comes in a recipe from Bengal for mango chutney. The lady who provided that exotic recipe became famous in "Society" for her Eastern wonders.

Today, apart from the cows which graze on Wanstead Common, there isn't a working farm animal within 20 miles of the centre of London. It was very different in the 1860s. Local shops were often supplied by local farmers. Cows grazed on what were then the outskirts of London. Asparagus grew in Deptford which is marked with an A on the map.

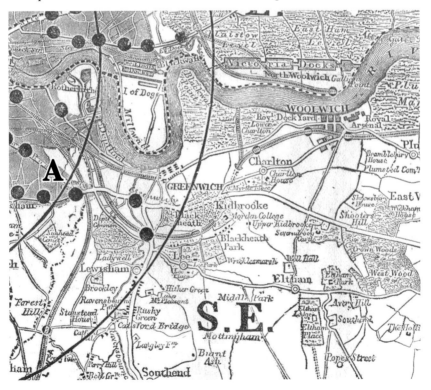

Cooking with a quill

But the fact produce was local did not mean it was never dodgy. Isabella worried about the freshness of eggs, for example. She wrote;

"In choosing eggs apply the tongue to the large end of the egg and if it feels warm, it is new and may be relied on as a fresh egg."

Try doing that in Tesco's or Sainsbury's!

Since there was no refrigeration, readers needed to know how to keep eggs fresh for weeks. Isabella could not rely on ice.

"Put the eggs into a cabbage net say 20 at a time and hold them in the water which must be kept boiling for 20 seconds. We have tried this method of preserving eggs and can vouch for its excellence; they will be found at the end of 2 or 3 months quite good enough for culinary purposes. Although the white may be a little tougher than that of a new laid egg, the yolk will be nearly the same."

Such eggs should not be allowed to touch each other.

Another way of preserving eggs was to "immerse them in lime water soon after they have been laid."

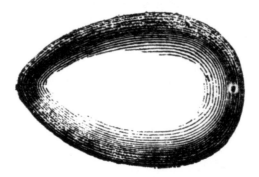

The 1850s did see many new appliances come to the market but Isabella's instructions on how to make caramel really bring home the difference between now then. A lump of sugar should be browned, and stock added. The mixture may be stirred she said "with the feather of a quill."

Isabella's medicine chest

The other remarkable difference between 1860 and now is the extent to which it was hard to get medical treatment even if you had ready money. Isabella advised the mistress of the house to have a well-stocked medical chest which should include;

Antimonial Wine, Antimonial Powder, Blister Compound, Blue Pill, Carbonate of Potash, Epsom Salts, Goulard's Extract, Compound Tincture of Camphor, Jalap in Powder, Opium powder and Laudanum, senna leaves, opodelioc, Sweet Spirits of Nitre, Turner's Cerate.

One does wonder if a Blue Pill is vital, why there is no need for a red, green or purple pill?

To us, it is striking that opium was considered as necessary as aspirin or deodorant would be now. Isabella, who was very cautious, did not think of warning against becoming addicted to it, even though both she and her publisher husband must have been aware of that other best seller - Thomas De Quincey's *Confessions of an Opium Eater.*

Goulard's Extract was sub acetate of lead. Turner's Cerate contained unsalted butter, yellow wax, olive oil and prepared calamine, ingredients. which have little significant therapeutic uses.

Specialised medical treatment around 1860

▼▼▼

Ingredients for one of the great best sellers.

The recipes are set out in a standardized form but one of the appealing things about the book is that Isabella collated so much and so varied information. Few chapters don't have a mix of myth, history and chemistry. And the first sections tell us about the social history of the time. The chapters on The Mistress, the Housekeeper and the Arrangement and Economy of the Kitchen give an insight into how well off Victorians ran their homes and lived their lives.

Then, Isabella offers general observations on each of the following subjects.

Stock and Soups
Vegetables
The Natural History of Fishes
Sauces, Pickles, Gravies and Forcemeats
Various Modes of Cooking Meat
Quadrupeds – beef and oxen
The sheep and the lamb
The common hog
The Calf
Birds – which, for some reason, included rabbits
Game
Puddings and Pastry
Creams, Jellies, Souffles, Omlets and Sweet Dishes
Preserves, Confectionery, Ices, Dessert Dishes
Milk Butter Cheese and Eggs
Beverages
Invalid Cookery
Dinners and Dining
The Rearing and Management of Children
The Doctor
Legal Memoranda

Making the recipes useful

Isabella was guiding her readers on how to cope in a complex and shifting society where very many longed to be upwardly mobile. I try to give a sense not just of her recipes but often of her interesting social comment. I provide linking materials to many short extracts of Isabella's book so that it is easy, I hope, for the reader to follow.

Though the book is famous as a cook book, Isabella did not often recommend a recipe. Out of 2000 recipes, she seems to have singled out a mere 40, saying they were good or excellent. I don't suggest that means she didn't think the other 1960 recipes were good, but Isabella was a careful writer and she must have highlighted these 40 for a good reason. I reproduce Mrs Beeton's Top 40 verbatim so that readers can experience – and try out – what Isabella believed was the very best.

Some readers have complained that the recipes of *The Book of Household Managment* are difficult to use today because all the measures are given in the then current imperial measures – pints, gallons, ounces etc. These have been converted into more user friendly measures for today to make the Top 40 more useful.

For historical interest, I have left in the cost as she reckoned it in 1861 and, then calculated what it would cost to cook the same dish today.

1 GALLON

$$= \quad 2/3$$

OF A KILOMETRE

Mrs Beeton's Top 40 recipes

On 40 recipes she added the note **very good, excellent or nice**.

Her top recipes fell into quite interesting groups.

Soups
Soup à la Cantatrice, an excellent soup very beneficial for the voice. 119

"Eggs and sago have always been deemed very beneficial to the chest and throat," Isabella said and noted that the Swedish nightingale Jennie Lind swore by this soup.

Vegetable Soup - Good and Cheap 161
A Good Mutton Soup 175

Isabella was generally pro-salad - but only one part of salad made it into her Top Forty.

Salads

Cucumber added – a very tasty addition to salad

Eggs
Ham omelet - a delicious breakfast dish 1457

Isabella often snipes at Victorian food manufacturers and wonders just what it is they put in their sauces. But she provided eight recipes for sauces in her Top 40.

Gravies, Pickles and Condiments

Jugged Gravy - excellent 211
Indian Pickle - very superior 451
Leamington sauce- (an excellent sauce) 459
Mixed Pickle - very good 471
Pickled Onions - very good 486
Salad Dressing - excellent 506
Tomato Sauce for Keeping - excellent 530
Pickled Walnuts - very good 534
White Sauce - good 537

In her long chapter on fish, Isabella is poetic about the mackerel's beauty (even when dead on the quay), but she doesn't note very good or excellent against one fish dish. Meat is very different. The lady was no veggie. She includes eight meat dishes she judges good or excellent.

Meat

Rib of Beef Bones - a pretty dish 644
Miniature round of Beef - an excellent dish for a small family 648
Sliced and Broiled Beef −a pretty dish 664
Toad in the hole - a Homely but Savoury Dish 701
Boiled Loin of Mutton - very excellent 729
Minced Veal - very good 889
Jugged Hare -very good 1051
Rolled Mutton − very good 1066

Vegetables

Baked Tomatoes - excellent 1158

By far the greatest number of excellent recipes come under the heading of puddings

Puddings

Another Good Short Crust 1211
Baked Apple Pudding 1231
Nesselrode Pudding - a fashionable iced pudding 1313
An Unrivalled Plum Pudding 1326
Christmas Plum Pudding - very good 1328
The Hidden Mountain - a very pretty supper dish 1148
Lemon Creams - very good 1445
Pineapple Fritters - An elegant dish 1472
Rice Snowballs - a pretty dish for juvenile suppers 1479
Compote of Apricots - an elegant dish 1521
To preserve cherries in syrup - very delicious 1529
Brillat Savarin's fondue - an excellent recipe 1644
A nice useful cake 1757
Sunderland Gingerbread nuts - an excellent recipe 1761
A very good seed cake 1776

Wines

Gooseberry Vinegar - an excellent recipe 1820
A very simple and easy method of making a very superior orange wine 1827

Diary of a Nobody

It is one of the oddities of the book that Isabella doesn't say much about wine at all. She never suggests, as a modern pundit might, that fondue would go well with a perky little Juracon, or beef with a second growth Pauillac from the sunny side of the hill.

I deduce from her favourite recipes that Isabella had a real sweet tooth!

And just as what Isabella tells us is revealing, what she does not mention is also interesting. The Victorians were obsessed with their digestion but did not seem too concerned about their teeth. Isabella never touches on teeth except when she discusses how to cope with babies teething. And there are no hygienic hints on when and how to use your toothbrush.

Victorian society was very class conscious. Mrs Beeton was writing for the growing middle class who lived in new, affordable London suburbs such as Islington and Streatham. It's a world which, some 40 years later was touchingly described in *Diary of a Nobody*.

"I cannot tell what induced me to do it, but I seized her round the waist, and we were silly enough to be executing a wild kind of polka when Sarah entered, grinning, and said: 'There is a man, mum, at the door who wants to know if you want any good coals.' Most annoyed at this. Spent the evening in answering, and tearing up again, the reply to the Mansion House, having left word with Sarah if Gowing or Cummings called we were not at home. Must consult Mr. Perkupp how to answer the Lord Mayor's invitation."

Old money, old aristocracy, "Society" knew how to run a house. But a girl who had no background needed to know the rules if she was not to embarrass herself or the all powerful master, her husband.

Isabella's first rule was that a woman had to be the general in her own house.

"She ought always to remember that she is the first and last, the Alpha and Omega, in the government of her establishment."

"As with the commander of an army, so it is with the mistress of a house. Of all those acquirements which more particularly belong to the feminine character, there are none which take a higher rank than a knowledge of household duties."

Isabella quoted *The Vicar of Wakefield* who lay down the law domestic.

"The modest virgin, the prudent wife and the careful matron are much more servicable in life than petticoated philosophers, blustering heroines or virago queens."

And while petticoated philosophers might lie in bed late, the Mistress had to be up early giving orders to her domestic troops. To do that properly the Mistress had to know which servant was meant to do precisely what. Etiquette was complex. A household could have a butler, footmen, underfootmen, valets, boys, grooms, housekeepers, under cooks, over cooks, corkers, porkers, housemaids, lady's maids – not to mention "the maid of all work". That really was a job.

Isabella set out the duties of all the ranks of servants, even those who looked after the horses. The distinctions she made tell us a great deal;

"The real duties of the butler are in the wine cellar; there he should be competent to advise his master as to the price and quality of the wine to be laid in."

In fiction, great butlers cannot be corrupted. One dreads to think how P.G Wodehouse's Jeeves would have swatted away a wine merchant who offered him a fiver to order an inferior claret for Bertie Wooster. But Isabella was more cynical.

Lard on the hair

"The position of butler is one of very great trust in the household. The butler's reputation will soon compensate for the absence of bribes from unprincipled wine merchants if he serves a generous and hospitable master. Nothing spreads more rapidly in society than the reputation of a good wine cellar."

Being cynical, Isabella added advice on how to make sure that the butler was keeping honest accounts – and not snaffling the best wines for himself in his pantry. Because butlers might get ideas above their station.

The butler did not get his hands dirty. The footman was the mucky one. "The footman is expected to rise early in order to get through all the dirty work before the family are stirring."

The footman cleaned the cutlery, the glasses and just about everything else.

The key domestic for the lady of the house was her maid – and she had to be a Jill of all trades.

"The lady's maid should be a tolerably expert milliner and dressmaker, a good hairdresser and possess some chemical knowledge of the cosmetics which the toilet table is supplied and use them with safety and effect."

One of the duties of the lady's maid was to be a hairdresser and hair restorer. Isabella offered advice on how "to promote the growth of hair". She recommended "equal quantities of olive oil and spirit of rosemary – a few drops of oil of nutmeg" which should be rubbed into the scalp.

"Hair should be washed in borax, 1/2 pint of olive oil and boiling water."

As always there was a need for stuff to put on the hair, but Isabella's Pomade sounds distinctly unappealing now.

To make Pomade for the Hair

INGREDIENTS ¼ lb lard, 2 pennyworth of castor oil; scent

Let the lard be unsalted; beat it up well; then add the castor oil and mix thoroughly together with a knife, adding a few drops of any scent that may be preferred.

Put the pomatum into pots which keep well covered to prevent it turning rancid

but society was not totally fixed – even below stairs.

"The position of the scullery maid is, not of course, one of high rank, nor is the payment for her services large. " But training would help. Isabella knew of one girl who was so determined that

" she showed herself so active and intelligent that she very quickly rose to the rank of kitchen maid; and from this, so great was her gastronomical genius, she became, in a short space of time one of the best woman cooks in England. After this, we think, it must be allowed that a cook, like a poet, nascitur non fit."

the servant problem

It was probably a bit idealistic of Isabella to assume her readers all had the Latin. But luckily, her husband also published phrase books of foreign languages which would have translated the tag as – a cook "is born, not made."

It shows how fluid society could be that Isabella warned footmen not to remind their masters when they made mistakes of etiquette, which nouveau riche masters were prone to. A 40 year old footman – and there were plenty of them – might well have seen more of society than his master who had just made a fortune in railway shares.

Isabella had no time for unjust snobs though;

"It is the custom of Society to abuse its servants, which lead matronly ladies and ladies just entertaining their probation in that honoured and honourable state to talk of servants, and we are told to wax eloquent over the greatest plague in life while taking their tea. It is another conviction of Society that the race of good servants has died out, at least in England. They complain that there is neither honesty, conscientiousness, nor the careful and industrious habits which distinguished the servants of our grandmothers and great grandmother and that domestics no longer know their place."

Isabella's dislike of snobbery is also clear when she praises that other famous Victorian woman, Florence Nightingale. Nightingale said children needed to see the light and to live in rooms "with no foul air." It was not just in the slums of St Giles you found foul air, Isabella sniped. "Belgravia and the squares have their north rooms where the rays of the sun never reach."

Isabella also commended Nightingale's advice on how bringing up children. "Don't treat your children like sick, don't dose them with tea. Let them eat meat and drink milk or half a glass of light beer."

Isabella then set out the timetable that a house should aspire to.

"Early rising is one of the most essential qualities of good Household management. If the mistress remains in bed, even for one extra hour, then domestics will become sluggards. The great Lord Chatham advised "I would have inscribed on the curtains of your bed and the walls of your chamber;

If you do not rise early, you can make progress in nothing."

"If the quality of early rising be of the first importance to the mistress, what must it be for the servant?"

Servants should rise by 6 a.m in the summer and 7 a.m. in the winter, so that by 8 a.m., Isabella decreed, the mistress could have her breakfast brought in. After she had eaten, she would hand out orders for the day. It was vital that the house was impeccably clean and that the staff knew precisely what meals they had to "dish up."

But the mistress should not just by the Commander of the Domestics. She had to also make sure she had some interesting "accomplishments."

"Unless the means of the mistress be very circumscribed, and she be obliged to devote a great deal of her time to making her children's clothes, and other economical pursuits, she should give some time to the pleasures of literature, the innocent delights of gardening and to the improvement of any special abilities for music, painting and other elegant arts which she may happily possess."

The fact that the lady of the house was accomplished was no reason for her to be uppity towards her lord and master.

"If the mistress be a wife, never let an account of her husband's failing pass her lips."

Or else!

"Good temper should be cultivated by every mistress."

Isabella then had sections on the etiquette of paying and receiving morning calls and a special section on condolence. This was part of what made her book so attractive to readers. She was giving advice on how to take the first steps into Society. Never speak ill of Society, Lady Bracknell, Oscar Wilde's magnificent madam warned, "only those who cannot get into it do that."

Passing the port properly

And one good way to enter into Society was to get a reputation for giving the perfect

dinner party

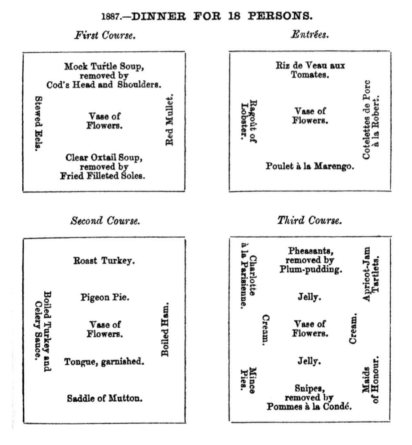

1887.—DINNER FOR 18 PERSONS.

First Course.

Mock Turtle Soup,
removed by
Cod's Head and Shoulders.

Stewed Eels.

Vase of
Flowers.

Red Mullet.

Clear Oxtail Soup,
removed by
Fried Filleted Soles.

Entrées.

Riz de Veau aux
Tomates.

Ragout of
Lobster.

Vase of
Flowers.

Cotelettes de Porc
à la Robert.

Poulet à la Marengo.

Second Course.

Roast Turkey.

Pigeon Pie.

Boiled Turkey and
Celery Sauce.

Vase of
Flowers.

Boiled Ham.

Tongue, garnished.

Saddle of Mutton.

Third Course.

Charlotte
à la Parisienne.

Pheasants,
removed by
Plum-pudding.

Apricot-Jam
Tartlets.

Jelly.

Cream.

Vase of
Flowers.

Cream.

Mince
Pies.

Jelly.

Maids
of Honour.

Snipes,
removed by
Pommes à la Condé.

But it could be tense, the perfect dinner party.

"The half hour before dinner has been considered as the great ordeal through which the mistress, in giving a dinner party, will either pass with flying colours or lose many of her laurels."

The long half hour

And verse captured that tension;

"How sad it is to sit and pine
The long half hour before we dine
Upon our watches oft to look
Then wonder at the clock and cook

And strive to laugh in spite of Fate
But laughter forced soon quits the room.
And leaves it in its former gloom
But lo, the dinner now appears
The object of our hopes and fears
The end of all our pain."

The good hostess had to make sure, however, that dinner parties did not go too far;

"Hospitality is a most excellent virtue but care must be taken
that the love of company does not become a prevailing passion
the habit is no longer hospitality but dissipation."

The moment when dissipation really happened was when the ladies retired and the men got down to the port, cigars and risqué jokes. Isabella was much too proper to discuss dirty jokes but she outlined what should happen after dessert.

Never gargle at dinner

The ladies retire

"When dinner is finished the dessert is placed on the table accompanied by finger glasses. It is the custom of some gentleman to wet a corner of the napkin. But the hostess whose behaviour will set the tone to all ladies present will merely wet the tips of her fingers which will serve all the purposes required. The French have a habit of gargling with the mouth; but it is a custom which no Englishwoman should in the slightest degree imitate."

Isabella went on to quote Dr Johnson on the British gentleman. "When he has drunk wine, but he is not improved, he is only not sensible of his defects." Isabella noted that "this is rather severe but there may be truth in it."

Manners had fortunately improved since the dissolutions of the 18th century.

"In former times when the bottle circulated freely among the guests it was necessary for the ladies to retire earlier than they do at present, for the gentlemen of the company soon became unfit to conduct themselves with that decorum which is essential in the presence of ladies."

But more "delicacy" and the fact that middle classes did not feel it essential to get drunk, made Victorian men less likely to disgrace themselves and embarrass the ever precious ladies. It also made it less likely they would knock over the very magnificent "tazza."

on which fruits and desserts were presented.

Revisions and editions

As part of my research, I have also looked at some of the revisions of Mrs Beeton. Perhaps the most interesting one is the 1960 version published by Jonathan Cape to mark the centenary of the first publication. It came out before the Swinging Sixties started to swing and the editors tried desperately to keep a genteel tone. But so much had changed. Few houses had any staff. At the start of the book there was a section on what would become a middle class obsession – how to buy property. There were also sections on interior design and on the latest gadgets. The editors had none of Isabella's reservations about new fangled gas cookers or dishwashers which were then beginning to appear. There was also far more sign of a multi cultural cuisine. Ironically the new edition removed most of the quirky details which made Isabella such a good read.

Having explained how to run a house and enter society, Isabella turned her attention to the kitchen. Her aim was to help readers become happy like maybe the two women below.

"Old folks at home."

In search of the perfect fruit and vegetable

Isabella wrote as the new science of food interested a newly educated middle class. They wanted food that was tasty but also nutritious. Many of her asides concern whether a particular food is good for you – and whether your stomach could take it. She was especially worried about the ability of ageing stomachs and included a section on cooking for invalids. Vegetables could be very bothersome as "inadequate stomachs" would not be able to digest them. But she had a solution for that.

Vegetables Reduced to Puree

"Persons in the flower of youth having healthy stomachs and leading active lives may eat all sorts of vegetables mostly without inconvenience save in excess. The digestive functions possess great energy during the period of youth. An old proverb says 'At twenty one, one can digest iron'. For aged persons, the sedentary or the delicate, it is quite otherwise. Those who generally digest vegetables with difficulty should eat them reduced to a pulp or puree that is to say with their skins and tough fibres removed. Subjected to this process vegetables which, when entire, would create flatulence or wind are then comparatively harmless."

Isabella was a great believer in making it easy for the reader.

"We would recommend that the young housekeeper, cook or whoever be engaged in the important task of 'getting ready' the dinner to follow pre-cisely the order in which the recipes are given. Thus let them first place on the table all the ingredients necessary; then the modus operandi or mode of preparation will be easily managed. By a careful reading of the recipes there will be not be the slightest difficulty in arranging a repast for any number of persons and an accurate notion will be gained of the **TIME**, the cooking of each dish will occupy, of the periods at which it is **SEASONABLE** as also of the **AVERAGE COST.**"

Heroes of cookery

And cost was an issue. Isabella added that you could decide or save money by using **BEST**, **MEDIUM** or **COMMON** stock.

As the phrase modus operandi suggests, Isabella assumed her readers would have some knowledge of Greek and Latin history. Today we're not so educated. Since she quotes many authors modern readers may not know I provide a summary of who they are. Many of them are not particularly known for their contributions to cooking.

Achilles "was adept at turning a spit."

Aesculapius, Greek doctor who is reckoned to be second only to Hippocrates.

Anacreon (563 – 474 BC) a Greek poet who praised wine and love.

Aristotle, the great philosopher, author of The Poetics and a very early scientist.

Cato, the great Roman orator who tried to save the Republic.

Diana, the goddess of the hunt.

Dioscordies, a Greek writer on plants who became influential at the time of the Renaissance.

Homer, Greek poet, author of The Iliad.

Nestor whose father and brother were killed by Heracles was brought up among the Gerenians – not geraniums – and later became leader of the Pylians against Troy.

His famous saying when Achilles gave him a prize was resigned. He said "Now I must leave this sort of thing to younger men and take the painful lesson of Old Age."

Plato, another great Greek philosopher, author of The Republic and of The Symposium. The Symposium was a dialogue set at an Athenian dinner party.

Pliny; there were actually two Plinys – the younger and the elder. They were prolific letter writers in Rome in the 1St century AD.

Theseus who was the grandson of the king of Troezen, proved himself a hero by lifting a huge boulder. The lad was sixteen at the time. One day his mother called Theseus to her side. It was time to tell him his father ruled a great kingdom. As Theseus believed his father was one of the gods, he was a bit miffed.

Thuyccicdes, Greek historian of the Persian wars.

Trimacalio, a Sicilian cook famous in the 1st century AD.

Ulysses who "excelled at lighting a fire" was one of Homer's heroes.

Xenophon, historian of the Anabasis.

Insipid stock

Of Stock

"It is on a good stock or a good stock and broth that excellence in cooking depends. If the preparation of this basis of the culinary art is entrusted to negligent or ignorant persons and the stock is not well skimmed," kitchen catastrophe will ensue.

"The theory of this part of Household Management may appear trifling but its practice is extensive and therefore it requires the best attention."

Isabella devoted four pages to stock. Bones were essential to good stock because "two ounces of them contain as much gelatine as one pound of meat; but in them this is so encased in the earthly substance that boiling water can dissolve only the surface of the whole bones. By breaking them, however, you can dissolve them more and by reducing those to paste or powder you can dissolve them entirely."

But gelatine had no taste at all. That was why it was necessary "to add meat to the pulverized bones because the osmasome contained in that makes the stock savoury."

Isabella advised "never wash meat because that will dilute its juices."

The meat had to be cut in small pieces, the bones had to be broken into pieces and tied in a bag and put in the stock pot. Isabella was firm about the scum which boiling all this would produce. "Do not let the stock boil because then one portion of the scum will be dissolved and the other will go to the bottom of the pot thus rendering it very difficult to obtain a clear broth."

Vegetables should be added. Then it was a question of time. "After 6 hours of slow and gentle simmering the stock is done." But it had to be tasted and then taken off the heat "or it will tend to insipidity."

Ever economical, she pointed out; "It is a great saving this to make use of the bones of meat which, in too many English families, are entirely wasted."

Isabella's Fruit and Veg

If only Eve had known how to stew apples

The Apple

On the subject of the Apple, which caused the downfall of Eve, Adam, not to mention the Fall and our expulsion from Garden of Eden, Isabella was unusually coy. All she says is "this useful fruit is mentioned in Holy Writ." There is no mention of fig leaves.

Isabella didn't usually censor herself like that. She was happier with Greek and Roman references to the apple. "Homer describes it as valuable." She noted that the Romans named some species of apples after their great families so there was the Apple Claudius and the Apple Manlius. It is perhaps odd that Caesar, the greatest Roman of them all, only had a salad named after him.

Perhaps it was because the apple had caused so much trouble for Woman and Mankind that it was hard on the digestion.

"As a food the apple cannot be considered to rank high, as more than half of it consists of water and the rest of its properties are not of the most nourishing. It is however as useful adjunct to other kinds of food and when cooked is esteemed as a slight laxative. Apples are a mostly a grateful food for the dyspeptic."

What is striking is that all Isabella's recipes assume apples must be cooked. She gave recipes for baked apple custard, buttered apple, flanc of apples, apple fritters, apple hedgehog, apple jelly, apples and rice, apples portuguese- they were served with cherries and apricot jam- apple snow, stewed apples and custard.

A recipe that is rarely seen today is apple soup.

The best apples, Isabella noted, were grown in New York but often by the time they had been shipped to Britain, they had rotted.

Aperient, dieuretic and deobstruent

The Asparagus

Isabella was more positive about.

"The plant not only acts as a wholesome and nutritious vegetable but also a diuretic, aperient and deobstruent," Isabella wrote. Of these words, the only one still in frequent use is *diuretic*.

"It belongs to the class of luxurious rather than necessary food. It is light and easily digested but not very nutritious. Intense quantities of it are raised for the London market at Mortlake and Deptford."

To a modern Londoner, this aside shows how much the city has changed. Deptford today is a rather depressed area where finding green is like finding a needle in a haystack. But in Victorian times, the land was amok with asparagus. At Kynarve Cove in Cornwall "there is an island called Asparagus Island," Isabella wrote, a perfect example of the asparagus epidemic.

She recommended boiled asparagus - and asparagus pudding which we would know these days as asparagus quiche.

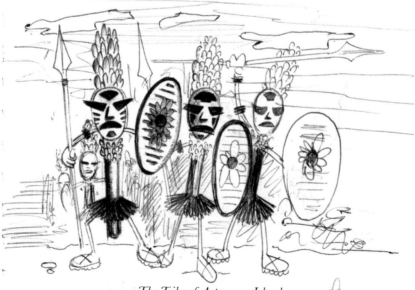

The Tribe of Asparagus Island

40

THE SECRETS OF ASPARAGUS ISLAND

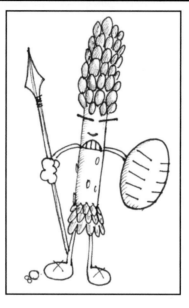

The asparagus had an intriguing relative in "the asparagus tribe" - the
sea kale. This vegetable had a backstory. "It had come into repute
in 1794." Sadly Isabella did not explain what had led to the sea kale
developing a reputation but, after 1794, "it is esteemed as one of the most
valuable esculents indigenous to Britain. It is so light that the most delicate
organizations may readily eat it."

Like aperient and deobstruent, words that Isabella often used, the word
"esculent" is now obsolete but it means delicious.

Isabella never neglected natural history and added that the flowers of the
sea-kale "form a favourite resort for bees."

"No knowledgeable person of either sex would ask for an interpretation of
asparagus," wrote Freud in *The Interpretation of Vegetables*, sorry, *of Dreams*.

The Cabbage God

The first vegetable Isabella rooted for with no reservation was

The cabbage

The cabbage did not just have a natural history but a spiritual one too. For, once upon a time, the cabbage was God.

"The Egyptians adored and raised altars to cabbages and the Greeks and Romans ascribed the most exalted virtues to them. The Roman sage, Cato affirmed that the cabbage cured all diseases and declared that its use allowed the Romans to live for 600 years without recourse to physicians. Unlike the apple and the asparagus, "the whole tribe" – of cabbages, not Romans – "is in general wholesome and nutritive." The reason was;

"The cabbage contains much vegetable albumen and several parts sulphur and nitrate of potash."

As a result, Isabella said "the cabbage is heavy and a long time digesting which has led to a belief that that it is very nourishing. It is only fit food for robust and active persons; the sedentary or delicate should carefully avoid it."

She said that the cabbage grew wild, with large yellow flowers, on the cliffs of Dover.

Her recipes for cabbage are rather basic – boiled cabbage or stewed red cabbage.

Its vegetable relation, the cauliflower, could upset the stomach even more dramatically.

"The cauliflower should be eaten moderately as it induces flatulence. People of weak constitutions and delicate stomachs should abstain from the cauliflower as much as possible."

Carrot whiskey

Carrots

The famous chemist, Sir Humphrey Davy, had analysed the carrot in detail. He said that the nutritive part of the carrot amounted to 98 parts in 1000. "It yields more spirit in the distillery than any other fruit or vegetable."

Which makes one wonder why carrot whisky has never been made.

On how easy it was to digest carrots, Isabella was silent.

Celery

This vegetable provoked digestion neurosis in the already digestively neurotic Victorians.

"It is extensively used by the Germans. In a raw state this plant does not suit weak stomachs; cooked it is less difficult of digestion although a large quantity should not be eaten."

She offered recipes for celery sauce, celery vinegar but not for braised celery.

The divine cucumber

The Cucumber

like the cabbage, went back to the beginnings of time.

"The antiquity of this fruit is very great. In the sacred writings we find that the people of Israel regretted it whilst sojourning in the desert." But perhaps that was a good thing as it "is difficult of digestion when eaten raw. In Egypt it is esteemed by the upper class natives as the most pleasant fruit they have."

I carried out extensive research – OK I rang my friend Jennifer Frazer who writes for the Jewish Chronicle – which revealed that Isabella was not quite right about the Bible and the cucumber. After consulting the rabbis who are on call for the Jewish Chronicle, Jennifer told me " OK, not Exodus but Numbers Chapter 11, and it's not cucumbers as we know them but the word used is "kishuim," which we know as courgettes. They also moan about fish, melons, leeks, onions and garlic. Does that help," Jennifer said. She also suggested that Moses' legions got bored with eating manna in the desert and so he created the pickled cucumber!

The Victorians also called cucumber the Musk Melon. Isabella noted that it was also "slightly laxative."

All this would have been surprised Oscar Wilde who made great play of the role of cucumber sandwiches in society. In *The Importance of Being Earnest* to impress his aunt, the formidable Lady Bracknell, Algernon wants his butler to provide her with cucumber sandwiches. Cucumber sandwiches are totally, completely, irrevocably respectable. The butler, Lane goes to Covent Garden but returns empty-handed. I quote what I believe is the only scene in world drama to centre on cucumber sandwiches.

LANE, THE BUTLER;   **There are no cucumbers, sir.**

ALGERNON;   **Not even for ready money, Lane?**

(Ready money was something Algernon never had)

LANE;   **Not even for ready money, sir.**

But by the end of the play, everyone seems to have got cucumber sandwiches.

Garlic

Today, garlic is the great demand. We believe it helps the heart and promotes a long life. In Germany, garlic pills are sold by the millions. But Isabella only mentions garlic once - and that is in connection with the Bengal Recipe for making mango chutney, one of her few non European recipes.

"The smell of this plant is generally considered offensive and it is the most acrimonious in its taste of the whole of the alliaceous tribe. It was introduced into England in 1548 from the shores of the Mediterranean and it was in greater repute with our ancestors than it is with ourselves."

The smell of this plant is generally considered offensive and it is the most acrimonious in its taste of the whole of the alliaceous tribe.

The Pope's vegetables

Haricots

Isabella always wanted her readers to have the latest scientific analysis and a hot topic was haricot beans. She tracked down a certain Mr Einhoff in the Agricultural and Chemical Laboratory in Scotland. He had subjected the haricot to every kind of chemical barrage known to science in the 1860s.

"From 3840 parts of kidney beans, Einhoff obtained 1805 parts of matter analogous to starch, 351 parts of animal vegetable matter and 799 parts of mucilage." Mucilage was fibre.

The haricot, Isabella complained, was unjustly neglected in the British kitchen.

And so was its cousin – the lentil.

Lentils

Today the lentil is one of the wonder pulses but, in Victorian times, it was far from respectable because eating lentils smacked of following the Pope.

"Although these vegetables are not much used in this country, yet in France and other Catholic countries, they form an excellent substitute for animal food during Lent and other maigre days."

Maigre days were not days of fasting, but days where faithful Catholics did not touch meat or fish. The Victorians were themselves very religious but inclined not to fast much. And the association with the Catholic Church damaged the good name of lentils, for Isabella explained; "As reformations are often carried beyond necessity possibly lentils may have fallen into disuse as an article of diet for fear that use of them might be considered a sign of popery."

How not to be poisoned

The mushroom

"These are common parasitical plants," Isabella wrote.

She was struck by how fast they could grow. "To spring up like a mushroom in the night" is a scriptural mode of expressing celerity – and this completely accords with all the observations that have been made concerning this curious class of plants."

Since Isabella's day, the mushroom has come to be seen as a phallic symbol.

There is then the only reference to a phallus I can find in the book. While she gave advice on how to cope with all kinds of medical conditions, erection problems were not amongst them. She quotes a Mr Sowerby who said;

"I have often placed specimens of the Phallus caninus by a window overnight and they were fully grown in the morning."

There were two mysteries to the mushroom – what made them grow so fast and also just why some were poisonous and some were edible.

Isabella noted that in Germany, Russia and Poland, many species of mushrooms grew wild and were eaten "but in Britain only two kinds were generally used."

"Generally they are difficult of digestion and by no means very nourishing. Many of them are of suspicious qualities. Even the same plant, it is affirmed may be innocent when young but noxious when it is old," she wrote.

"Nearly all the poisonous kinds are brown and have in general a rank and putrid smell. Edible mushrooms are found in closely fed pastures but seldom grow in woods where most of the poisonous sorts are to be found."

"Some species which are perfectly harmless when raised in open meadows and pasture land, when they happen to grow in contact with stagnant water or putrescent animal and vegetable substances, become virulently poisonous."

have you ever seen one of these before, madam?

Isabella was much taken with reports from New Zealand, which was then a very new colony – the Maoris were only persuaded to sign it away to the great white Queen Victoria in 1840. The report was of "a long fungus which grows from the head of a caterpillar and forms a horn as it were and is called Spheria Robertsii."

The lack of refrigeration made the Victorians clever at preserving. Today we rarely dry mushrooms and, then, hope to bring them back to normal. Mushrooms could be dried by peeling the skin off, laying them on paper to dry and then placing them in a paper bag. They would shrivel but the mushroom could be inflated back to its usual size by being soaked in cold gravy and then simmered.

Isabella had recipes for baked mushrooms, broiled or grilled mushrooms, stewed mushroom and stewed mushroom in gravy, but what really made the mushroom magical was when it was used to make sauces and ketchup. She had recipes for white mushroom sauce – to serve with fowl and ketchup.

They could be picked in meadows between September and October.

Smelly leeks and sleepy lettuce

Bewail The Leek

Like the cucumber, this vegetable "was bewailed by the Israelites in their journey through the desert". Isabella warned that it should be very well boiled "to prevent its tainting the breath."

The Lemon

"Lemons were only known to the Romans at a very late period and, at first, were only used to keep moths from their garments; their acidity was so unpleasant to them. In the time of Pliny, the lemon was hardly known except as an excellent counter poison."

But Isabella thought the lemon had many possibilities and gave recipes for lemon mincemeat, lemon cheesecake, lemon dumplings, baked lemon pudding, boiled lemon pudding and Manchester pudding whose key ingredients were "lemon peel and brandy."

Lemons didn't just have to be eaten.

"The juice of the fruit makes one of our popular and refreshing beverages – lemonade. It may be freely partaken by bilious and sanguine temperaments but persons with irritable stomachs should avoid it on account of its acidity".

The Lettuce

The leaf had magical properties which were known to the Greeks.

"It possesses a narcotic virtue noticed by ancient physicians – and even in our day a lettuce supper is deemed conducive to repose."

No cheese please, we're British

Onions and Onion Soup

Like the cabbage, the onion had a spiritual history.

"This plant was erected into an object of worship by the idolatrous Egyptians 2000 years before the Christian era."

This was strange because the onion led to something the cabbage was innocent of. "The onion left "such a disagreeable odour to the breath" but she did offer a simple cure – chewing a little raw parsley.

Isabella was always conscious of cost. When it came to Onion Soup, she offered her readers either Luxury Onion Soup or Cheap Onion Soup. The price difference was huge. Onion Soup for 6 cost a shilling, but cheap onion soup would only be 4 pennies, a third of the price. The cheaper variety did not have cream or stock no 105, an ingredient she seemed to swear by.

The notion of French onion soup with cheese was not mentioned.

But even the cheapest onion soup was more expensive than a soup I feel I have to comment on because of its name - ***Prince of Wales Soup***. This was made of turnips and veal stock. "The soup was invented by a philanthropic friend of the editress and was to be distributed among the poor of a considerable village when the Prince attained his majority in 9th November 1859." Isabella pointed out, quoting her own *Dictionary of Universal Information*, that "British princes attain their majority in their 18th year while mortals of ordinary rank do not arrive at the until their 21st ."

Unlike Prince Charles, the current Prince of Wales, Victoria's eldest son had no organic-veggie tendencies. He liked to stuff himself with roast beef and, as far as know, never had a body detox or colonic irritation – sorry irrigation!

Don't feed parsley to your parrot

Parsley

Isabella gave a potted history of parsley in the ancient world.

"According to Homer's Iliad warriors fed their chariot steeds on parsley. Among the Greeks a crown of parsley was awarded both in the Nemenas and Isthmian games and the voluptuous Anacreon pronounced this beautiful herb the emblem of joy and festivity."

Here Isabella made one of her rare jokes;

"We learn from mythology parsley was used to adorn the head of a hero – no less than Hercules – and we moderns use it to decorate the head of a calf."

No less!

"Its flavour is very agreeable in soups," she said. Then came a devastating piece of information. "Although to rabbits, hares and sheep it is a luxury, to parrots it is a poison."

I have tried to check this extraordinary claim and on Google discovered that the best vet advice is, indeed, to use parsley very sparingly with your parrot feed.

Dr. Dave McCluggage, a highly respected holistic veterinarian of Colorado, juices different combinations of health-giving fruits and vegetables for his parrot family, as well as for his human family. He recommends selecting a parrot's favorite fruit or vegetable for juicing. He says that apples are always a good choice and he also recommends carrots, kale, spinach and other healthful fruits and vegetables.

It certainly offers an interesting insight into Monty Python's famous dead parrot sketch!

Horns, Marlborough, grey, purple and Birds' Eye

The Pea

Unusually Isabella contradicted herself on the matter of the pea.

In the section on vegetables she noted;

"The pea was well known to the Romans and probably first introduced to Britain at an early period for we find it mentioned by Lydgate, a poet of the 15th century, as being hawked around London. They seem to have fallen out of use for a considerable time. Fuller tells us they were brought from Holland and were accounted for "fit dainties for ladies they came so far and dear.""

But she added in a later section;

"In this country the pea has been grown from time immemorial."

She was, as often, fascinated by the many varieties and listed the early grey pea, the late grey, the purple grey, the Marlborough grey and the horn grey.

There were more varieties of pea than recipes for them, as all Isabella had to offer by way of cooking peas was boiled peas, stewed peas and peas à la Française which meant just sautéing them with a knob of butter. She added a wry note on

The Wood Pea

"The wood pea or heath pea is found in the heaths of Scotland and the Highlanders of that country are extremely partial to them and dry and chew them to give a greater relish to their whisky. They also regard them as good against chest complaints."

The suspicious potato

The Potato – and its paradoxes

Isabella was not always consistent - and this shows in her very contradictory account of the virtues and vices of the potato. "Next to the cereals, the potato is the most valuable plant for the production of human food." Of a thousand parts of the potato, Sir Humphrey Davy found about a fourth nutritive. Isabella's Scottish food chemist, Mr Finberg, had completed an even more flattering analysis of the nutritional value of the potato.

One of the pleasures of reading her book is the pleasure Isabella takes in describing different varieties of a vegetable.

"The Shaw is one of the most esteemed of the early potatoes. The Lancashire Pink is also a good potato." So was the Tartan, or kilted, potato.

Potato starch was even a work of art. "It is beautiful and it is an aliment which can not be too generally used as much on account of its wholesomeness as well as its cheapness." She even had a recipe for what she called potato snow, hot flakes of the tuber.

And one did not just have to eat the tubers - for she had evidence that "potatoes will clean linen as well as soap."

But it would be wrong to imagine Isabella was wholly pro-potato. She has 28 separate entries on potatoes and, in some, she condemns the entire family as if they could poison half the population. It seems a bit extreme to suggest that the potato can have criminal intent but she wrote;

"The whole of the family are suspicious; a great many are narcotic and many are deleterious. The leaves are narcotic generally."

But on one aspect of the potato, Isabella was adamant;

"It is generally supposed that the water in which potatoes are boiled is injurious and instances are recorded in which cattle having drunk it were seriously affected." The wise farmer never used the water which potatoes had been boiled in to feed animals.

Relish the radish but not too much

Radishes

Isabella was not ambivalent about; she pointed out

"they do not agree with people except those who are in good health and have active digestive powers for their difficult of digestion and cause flatulency and wind and are the cause of headaches when eaten to excess."

The horseradish Isabella was much more positive about. It "is highly stimulant and exciting to the stomach. It has been recommended in chronic rheumatism, palsy dropsical complaints and in cases of enfeebled digestion. It is one of the most powerful excitants and antiscorbutics we have."

I can find no trace of the Navy, however, making sailors eat horseradish to prevent scurvy.

The horseradish contained 30% sulphur and, while that was good for the stomach, it was hard on the dishes. The sulphur, Isabella pointed out, leads "the metal vessels into which the radish is distilled to turn a black colour."

Isabella also commented on how to keep horseradish.

"On account of the great volatility of its oil, it should never be preserved by drying but should be kept moist by being buried in the sand.

So rapidly does its volatile oil evaporate that even when scraped for the table it almost immediately spoils by exposure to the air."

**Isabella would probably now like you to guess
who the beard below belonged to!**

CENSORED
. . .

The poetry of salad

The Scarcity of Salads in England

Isabella blamed that sad fact on history. She pointed out that in Henry VIII's day there were no salads grown in England. Before he divorced Catharine of Aragon and started on his merry go round of six wives – divorced, beheaded, died, divorced, beheaded, survived - goes the old rhyme about the fates of Catharine of Aragon, Anne Boleyn, Jane Seymour, Anne of Cleves, Katherine Howard and Katharine Parr - Henry seems to have been a considerate husband.

"Queen Catherine herself, with all her royalty, could not procure a salad of English growth for her dinner. The king was obliged to mend this state of affairs and send to Holland for a gardener in order to cultivate pot herbs in the growth of which England is now not far behind any other country".

Not that it saved the marriage.

A salad for a saint

Isabella pointed out that the Rev Sydney Smith, the witty cannon of St Paul's, became poetic at the thought of salad. Isabella prayed that readers "May they find the flavour equal to the rhyme."

> **Two large potatoes passed through kitchen sieve,**
> **Smoothness and softness to the salad give**
> **Of mordant mustard add a single spoon**
> **Distrust the condiment that bites too soon;**
> **But deem it not, thou man of salt, a fault**
> **To add a double quantity of salt;**
> **Four times the spoon with oil of Lucca crown,**
> **And twice with vinegar procured from 'town';**
> **True flavour needs it and your poet begs**
> **The pounded yellow of two well-boil'd eggs.**
> **Let onion's atoms lurk within the bowl,**
> **And, scarce suspected, animate the whole;**
> **And, lastly, in the flavour'd compound, too**
> **A magic spoonful of anchovy sauce.**
> **Oh great and glorious, and herbaceous treat,**
> **'Twould tempt the dying anchorite to eat,**
> **Back to the world he'd turn his weary soul**
> **And plunge his fingers in the salad bowl.**

Henry VIII

(Who tried to bring salads to Britain)

Rich man and poor man's spinach

And maybe saints, like the anchorite, were worried about their complexion.

"Savacerian recommends (salads) to all who place confidence in him.
It refreshes without exciting – and he has a theory that it makes people
younger."

Spinach

was not a vegetable Isabella became that poetical about, despite tracing it
back to ancient Persia.

The leaves were shaped like worms, she sniped.

"It is not very nutritious but is very easily digested. It is very light and
laxative. Wonderful properties have been ascribed to spinach. Plainly
dressed it is a resource for the poor; prepared luxuriantly, it is a choice dish
for the rich."

She went on to give a recipe for dressing spinach richly, "luxuriantly in the
manner of the French" with good butter and nutmeg.

The love apple can bite

Tomato

"The plant which bears this fruit is a native of South America and takes its name from a Portuguese word," Isabella said.

The Victorians also called the tomato the love apple. She never mentions the reason but it seems that it was considered an aphrodisiac.

 But it was hard to be romantic after reading Isabella on the tomato's chemistry.

"The tomato has been found to contain a particular acid, a volatile oil, a brown very fragrant extracto-resinous matter, a vegeto-mineral matter, muco-saccharine, some salts and, in all probability, an alkaloid. The whole plant has a disagreeable odour and its juice, subjected to the action of the fire, emits a vapour so powerful as to cause vertigo and vomiting."

The trick was to eat it, not smell it nor distil its oil.

Today the tomato is eaten in salad but the Victorians were advised to pickle it, stew it, ketchup it and turn it into sauce by adding garlic, shallots, capsicum and other stuff.

Isabella added a section on

The Tomato Medicinal

"Dr Bennett, a professor of some celebrity, considers it to be an invaluable article of diet and ascribes to it very important medicinal properties. He declares that the tomato is one of the most powerful deobstruents of the materia medica; and that in all afflictions of the liver and other organs where calomel is indicated, it is probably the most effective and least harmful remedial agent known to the profession. He has treated diarrhea with this article alone and that, when used as an article of diet, it is almost a sovereign remedy for dyspepsia and indigestion."

The Truffle

Isabella claimed a professor had said "meats with truffles are the most distinguished dishes that opulence can offer the epicure."

But, she warned, "truffles are stimulating and heating. Weak stomachs cannot digest them easily. They should be eaten sparingly. Their wholesomeness is perhaps questionable."

For once Isabella did not give a price for truffles because they "are not often bought in this country."

But she was fascinated by their mystery.

"The truffle belongs to the family of the mushroom. It is certain that the truffle must contain an organ of reproduction. Yet notwithstanding all the efforts of art and science it has been impossible to subject them to a regular culture."

So in France, Italy and Britain, people had to root the truffles out of the ground where they lay buried. . Peasants used pigs in the hunt, but Isabella did not explain how the middle classes went hunting for the truffles. As we shall see when she discusses pigs, she believed hunting truffles was a way pigs kept sane.

Isabella knew truffles were a dish for the rich and gave instructions on how to dress truffles with champagne. The champagne was not completely necessary because she also had a recipe for truffles à l'italienne which required just cayenne pepper and gravy.

"Upon analysis truffles are found to contain not only the usual components of the vegetable kingdom such as carbon, oxygen and hydrogen but also a large proportion of nitrogen; from which they approach more nearly to the nature of animal flesh. It was long ago observed by Dr (Erasmus) Darwin that all the mushrooms cooked at our tables as well as those used for ketchup possessed an animal flavour."

Turnips are not for the tropics

The Turnip

"Good turnips are delicate in texture, firm and sweet. The best sort contain a sweet juicy mucilage uniting with the aroma a slightly acid quality which is completely neutralized by cooking."

"It is useful in the regimen of persons afflicted with chronic visceral irritations. The turnip only creates flatulency when it is soft, porous and stringy. It is consequently bad."

Isabella distinguished between different kinds of turnip. "The Swede is the largest variety but is too coarse for the table." Boiled turnips, cooked in coriander, went well with lamb, she said.

"Ducks stuffed with turnips have been highly appreciated."

The Germans, she noted, simmered their turnips in butter. It was also tasty to add a little mustard.

In India and other hot climates, however, the turnip became tasteless.

The prophet of pasta

Maize and Macaroni

Isabella had a journalistic disappointment when it came to maize.

"William Cobbett, the English radical writer and politician, was a great cultivator and admirer of maize and constantly ate it as a vegetable boiled. We believe he had a special recipe for it but we have been unable to lay our hands on it."

Isabella did not like failing to get her sources but she was able to offer a bit of high society gossip.

"Mr Buchanan, the present president of the United States, was in the habit, when ambassador here, of receiving a supply of Indian corns in hermetically sealed cases."

Isabella's husband was also a fan of maize. "The publisher Mr Beeton found it to combine the excellence of the young green pea and the finest asparagus, but he felt slightly awkward in holding the large ear in one hand while the other had to be employed it cutting off the delicate green grains."

And if maize was for the elite, macaroni was very different.

Macaroni

"This is the favourite food of Italy where especially among the Neapolitans it is regarded as the staff of life."

And the British should learn from the Italians.

"As it is both wholesome and nutritious it ought to be much more used by all classes in Britain than it is."

Isabella proved to be right. Maize we hardly ever eat now but pasta rules the world.

B

E

E

F

"Beef is truly the king of the kitchen"

Beef with everything and everything with beef

In her opening remarks on meat, even though she was the champion of refinement, Isabella praised raw meat;

"Brillat Savarin says that raw flesh has but one inconvenience – from its viscousness it attaches itself to the teeth."

Brillat Savarin told the story of a Croatian captain who didn't think meat had to be cooked.

"When we are campaigning and get hungry, we knock over the first animal we find, cut off a steak, powder it with salt which we always have in the sabretasche, put it under the saddle, gallop over it for a half a mile and then dine like princes."

When our ancestors first discovered fire, "the meat cooked on the coal would become somewhat befouled." Coal steak was not very nice and that led to the invention of the spit. But progress, Isabella believed, stopped there for centuries.

"In Homer's time, the art of cookery had not advanced much beyond grilling for we read in the Iliad how the great Achilles and his friend Patroclus regaled the three Grecian leaders on bread, wine and broiled meat. It is noticeable that Homer does not speak of broiled meat anywhere in his poems."

But Homer did not have the advantages Moses had who, according to Isabella, did not just bring the Jews out of Egypt, but also introduced them to kettles.

"And in one of these Esau's mess of pottage, for which he sold his birthright, must have been prepared."

Science now made it possible to be very precise about how to cook meat.

"The philosophy of frying consists in this, that liquids subjected to the action of fire do not all receive the same quantity of heat."

One could easily dip a finger into boiling wine but not into boiling water, she pointed out. Given her fears about digestion it is hardly surprising that Isabella was passionate about rooting out bad meat.

"Nothing can be more poisonous than such abominable carrion. The flesh of animals slaughtered while under depression of vital energy has a diminished tendency to stiffen after death, it presents an unusually blue appearance and has a faint and slightly sour smell."

Isabella also had an interesting observation to make which says much about her eye and ear for class distinctions. In her introduction to meat, she noted that while the animals' names are Saxon – ox, beef, sheep - the names of the dishes are Norman.

Beef is supposed to be the heart of British identity, Isabella said.

"Roast beef has long been a national dish in England. In most of our patriotic songs it is contrasted with the fricasseed frogs popularly supposed to be the exclusive diet of French men."

O the roast beef of Old England !

And O the old English roast beef !

"This national chorus is appealed to whenever a song writer wishes to account for the valour displayed by Englishmen on land or sea."

The battle of Waterloo was not won on the playing fields of Eton but in the kitchens!

Comments on beef as the symbol of Britain are peppered throughout the book, and at one point, Isabella does a fancy number of pirouettes on;

The origins of the word "Sirloin"

"The loin of beef is said to have been knighted by King Charles II at Friday Hall, Chingford. The Merry Monarch returned to this hospital mansion from Epping Forest literally hungry as a hunter and beheld with a delight a huge loin of beef steaming on the table."

"A noble joint," said Charles, "it shall have a title." Drawing his sword he raised it above the meat and cried "Loin we dub thee knight. Henceforth be Sir Loin."

"It is perhaps a pity to spoil so noble a story but the interests of truth demand that we declare sirloin is probably a corruption of sirloin, above the loin."

And there was even a grander version of the sirloin, Isabella said.

Ye Olde Baron of Beef.

"The baron of beef which consists of two sirloins was a favourite dish of our ancestors. It was not often seen because it was part of a whole requiring "the grim boar's head and Christmas pie as supporters." It was stirring feudal and bloody stuff. In Scotland when a lord's son came of age, even the baron of beef couldn't feed all those who were invited to the feast.

"A whole ox was therefore generally roasted over a fire built up of huge logs. We may here mention that an ox was roasted entire on the frozen Thames in the early part of the present century."

greed is good. So is goose.

Isabella quoted Sir Walter Scott's ode to a baron of beef;

Then was brought in the lusty brawn
By old blue coated serving man
Then the grim boar's head frown'd on high
Crested with bays and rosemary.
Well can the green garbed ranger tell
How, when and where this monster fell
What dogs before his death he tore,
And all the baiting of the boar;
While round the merry wassel bowl
Garnish'd with ribbons, blithe did trowl
There the huge sirloin reek'd; hard by
Plum porridge stood and Christmas pie
Nor failed Scotland to produced
At such high tide her savoury goose.

It shows how much Isabella loved beef that there are 79 recipes for beef. These ranged from very cheap recipes for broiled beef bones to beef à la mode which involved "clod of beef", fried ox feet to beef steaks with oyster sauce. She even gave one for Steak and Chips, which she called Biftek aux Pommes des Terres mode Francaise.

The French made far too extravagant claims for their own beef, however.

A Frenchman's Boeuf

Isabella quoted an authority in Paris who said beef " is an exhaustless mine in the hands of a skilful artist and is truly the king of the kitchen. Without it, no soup, no gravy and its absence would produce almost a famine in the civilized world."

Isabella offers interesting background to the perennial farming rivalries between England and France. Patriotically, she said "it is generally admitted the beef of France is greatly inferior to the beef of England." This was because French grass was not as good. But there was a French authority who beefed about this as English pride and vanity. Isabella socked back;

"We should not deign to notice it if it had occurred in a work of small pretensions but Mr Curmer's book professes to be a complete exposition of the scientific principles of cookery and holds a high rank in the didactic literature of France. We half suspected that Mr Curmer obtained his knowledge of English beef in the same way as the poor Frenchman in Mr Lewis' *Physiology of Common Life*."

In that book there is the following exchange.

Frenchman;

"I have been two times in England but I nevere find the bif so superior to ours."

His English audience was not convinced.

"But I do find it very convenient that they bring it on leetle pieces of stick or one penny but I do not find the bif superieure."

"Good Heavens, sir, you have been eating cat meat,"

replied the Londoner who knew just what was sold on the little sticks.

Sadly Isabella did not reveal the Frenchman's reactions.

Isabella concluded her footnote with a mixture of flattery and patriotism

"No, Mr Curmer, we are ready to acknowledge the superiority of your cookery but we have long since made up our minds as to the inferiority of your raw material."

memorandum on roasting, grilling and boiling

It was perhaps as a result of that feeling that Isabella's wonderfully named "Memoranda in Roasting" relied very heavily on French experts.

Such memos were needed because so many cooks were rubbish at roasting. In one way that was very understandable because it was hard to control the temperature of an oven in the 1850s. "A radiant fire throughout the operation is absolutely necessary to obtain a good result."

But some incompetents could never manage to keep the fire radiant enough. "Some cooks always fail in their roasting," Isabella noted. And she quoted one of her many French authorities. He said "that anybody can learn how to cook but one must be born a roaster."

As ever, Isabella offered scientific advice. She quoted Liebig who pointed out that you could roast poultry at 130 degrees, but that beef needed a minimum of 158 degrees. "This depends on the greater amount of blood which beef contains and the colouring matter of blood not being coaguable at less than 158 degrees."

The French had another great skill, she did admit.

"The French are noted for their skill in making forcemeats; one of the principal causes of their superiority being that they pound all the ingredients so diligently. Anyone with the slightest pretension to refined cookery must in this particular follow the example of our friends across the Channel."

But while the French might know how to roast and make forcemeats, they could not compete with Essex farmers when it came to producing veal.

The Calf

Isabella could not refrain from mentioning the golden calf of antiquity. The prophet Hosea, she banged on, "is full of denunciations of calf worship in Israel and alludes to the custom of kissing those idols."

She also quoted, but did not name, a French authority who claimed veal lent itself "to so many metamorphoses it may be called without exaggeration the chameleon of the kitchen."

But most of Isabella's notes on veal and the calf are more down to earth. The calf benefited from the milk of the cow's kindness.

"The affection and solicitude which the cow evinces for her offspring is more human in its tenderness and intensity."

Isabella noted that Britain was more civilized than some countries whose inhabitants had "vitiated appetites" and killed the poor calf in its first days. "We are happy to say that in this country the taste for very young veal has entirely gone out and "Staggering Bob" as the poor little animal was called in the language of the shambles, is no longer to be met with."

The slaughtering of calves was also more humane. "There was no species of slaughtering in this country so inhuman and disgraceful as that, till very lately, employed in killing this poor animal when under the plea of making the flesh white, the calf was bled day by day, until when the final hour came, the animal was unable to stand. This inhumanity is now, we believe, everywhere abolished."

The Victorians loved their veal and Isabella gave recipes for baked veal, roast breast of veal, veal cake, boiled calf's feet, fricasseed calf feet, six recipes for calf's head, veal cutlets, which she recommended should be done as a schnitzel, as well as hashed calf's head, veal sausages, veal and ham pie and minced veal and macaroni.

Her last word on veal, though, was yet another poke in the eye for the French.

"Essex farmers have obtained a celebrity for fattening calves better than any others in England where they are plentifully supplied with milk. A thing impossible to be done in the immediate neighbourhood of London," Isabella noted. And one impossible for French farmers to compete with.

Guzzle the gizzards

It was part of the less squeamish Victorian attitudes that they were ready to eat every bit of the animal. Isabella included an entry on

Marrow Bones

"Have the bones sawed nearly into convenient slices," she urged. Then, place the bones prettily dressed in a pan and heat them till you could scrape out the marrow, put it on toast and enjoy.

The tongue

The Victorians were also partial to tongue. But Isabella worried about just what kind of tongues were being offered by butchers. (Like butlers, butchers were potentially dodgy and had to be watched!)

"Dr Carpenter says that among lower animals the instinctive perceptions connected with this sense are much more remarkable than our own thus an omnivorous monkey will rarely touch fruits of a poisonous character although their taste may be agreeable. However man's instinct has decided that ox tongue is better than horse tongue. Yet the latter is frequently substituted for the former by dishonest dealers. The horse tongue may be readily distinguished by a spoon like expansion at the end."

So there was no reason the housewife should be fooled by dishonest butchers.

Pigs and Hogs

Isabella offered a vast range of recipes for pork – some are now forgotten, such as Roast Griskin of Pork, Pigs Cheeks and Pig Pettitoes.

Isabella noted there were several remarkable species of pigs in Norway and Sardinia that did not have cloven hoofs.

A close reading of the Bible suggested Jews were hypocritical about pigs, "for unless they ate pork it is difficult to conceive for what purpose they kept droves of swine." Her authority was Matthew xviii.32 which said, "when Jesus was in Galilee and the devils cast out, two men were permitted to enter the herd of swine that were feeding on the hills surrounding the Sea of Galilee."

But she approved of kosher laws because, in a very hot climate, "where vigorous exercise could seldom be taken it was easy to produce disease and especially cutaneous afflictions; indeed, in this light, as a code of sanitary ethics, the Book of Leviticus is the most admirable system ever conceived for man's benefit."

She noted that in ancient Egypt people were only permitted to eat pig once a year on the feast of the moon. There might be gods who came down to look after sheep but Isabella could find no instance of any divine being coming to earth to be a swineherd. Given her views on the hygiene of the pig, that was not surprising.

"From the grossness of his feeding, the large amount he consumes, his gluttonous way of eating it, from his slothful habits, the pig is particularly liable to disease."

The diseases are many. The pig is liable to suffer especially "from indigestion, heartburn and afflictions of the skin."

But the pig's brain "teaches him to seek relief and medicine." She noted that the pig "resorts to a tree to scratch his skin with the bark.

In his fine comic novels about Blandings Castle, P.G Wodehouse wrote about Clarence, the Earl of Emsworth and the owner of the Castle. His sisters nagged him all the time and could not understand his devotion to his superlative pig of pigs, The Empress of Blandings. She was able to consume 12000 calories a day which, according to Wodehouse, leading pig-ologists recommended was the minimum a growing pig needed to keep growing till it was shaped like a splendid balloon. Writing in the elegant 1920s, Wodehouse would never suggest that the Empress ever farted, though she did once get the hiccups. This tragedy was due to her guzzling 500 pages of paper on which Clarence's brother had written his memoirs.

Jeeves, Wooster and dog

let us praise hashed mutton

Sheep and Lambs

With her fondness for the Bible, Isabella noted that the lamb was perhaps the first animal sacrifice. She gave a brief account of the Passover meal where lamb has to be eaten with unleavened bread and bitter herbs "with the loins girded, the staff in the hand, the shoes on the feet. On extraordinary occasions vast quantities of sheep were sacrificed at once so Solomon, on completion of the temple, offered sheep and oxen that could not be told or numbered for multitude."

The Greeks didn't just use lamb in kebabs either. Isabella noted that 15th century alchemists claimed the Golden Fleece had been written on sheepskin.

As part of her mission to give the history behind the food, Isabella told a story about a wealthy landowner.

"How many sheep have you on your estate," asked Prince Esterhazy of the Duke of Argyll.

"I have not the most remote idea," replied the Duke, "but I know the shepherds number several thousand."

She delighted in the different breeds of sheep and claimed the tenderest sheep in Britain came from Banstead. And the best mutton? "The mutton of Sheep Down breed of mutton is highly valued for its delicate flavour."

But one did not have to only buy the best cuts. One of her many recipes that she praised for being economical was that for hashed mutton.

"Many persons express a decided aversion to hashed mutton and, doubtless, this dislike has arisen from the fact that they have unfortunately never been served the dish properly. Done properly the meat is tender. Then hashed mutton is by no means to be despised and is infinitely more wholesome and appetising than the cold leg or shoulder, of which fathers and husbands and their bachelor friends stand in such awe."

What did men know, after all?

ode to a sheep

Between her recipes for boiled neck of mutton and mutton scallops, Isabella pointed out that Shakespeare often compared men to sheep and she included a number of poems praising sheep.

Heavy and dripping to the breezy brow
Slow move the harmless race; where, as they spread
Their swelling treasures to the sunny ray
Inly disturbed and wondering what this wild
Outrageous tumult means, their loud complaints
The country fill, and toss'd from rock to rock
Incessant bleating run around the hills.

Robbie Burns' sad sheep

North of the border, the patron saint of haggis, Robert Burns, was very fond of his sheep Poor Maisie.

I wish she was a sheep o sense
An could behave herself with mense
I'll say 't she never brak a fence
Through thieving greed.

Scotland had also provided the most literate shepherd ever. James Hogg, she said, "was perhaps the most remarkable man that ever wore the maud of a shepherd. Under the garb, aspect and bearing of a rude peasant," she noted – and Hogg could apparently be very rude- "the world soon discovered a true poet." Hogg wrote *The Shepherd's Calendar*.

Of all the recipes the most intriguing perhaps was to dress a sheep's head. This was Isabella noted a Scottish dish.

"The village of Dudingston which stands within a mile of Edinburgh town was celebrated for this homely Scottish dish. In the summer many opulent citizens used to resort to this place to solace themselves over singed sheep's head, boiled or baked."

The girl who didn't eat sheep

Strange Tails

The only tail that Isabella gives a recipe for is ox tail but that did not stop her adding a note on animal tails in general.

"Naturalists cannot explain the uses of some of the strange tails of animals. In Egyptian and Syrian sheep, for instance, the tail grows so large that it cannot is not infrequently supported upon a sort of little cart in order to prevent an inconvenience to the animal. This monstrous appendage sometimes attains a weight of 70, or even 100 pounds."

Squeamish No

The Victorians were less squeamish about offal than we tend to be. They might worry about their guts and their digestion but they did not turn down tripe, calf's feet, calf head, trotters, liver and bacon, kidneys, marrow bones. What shows their willingness to eat anything just about is Isabella's recipe

For dressing a Bullock's Heart.

Ingredients 1 heart, stuffing of veal forcemeat.

"Put the heart into warm water to soak for 2 hours, then wipe it well with a cloth and after cutting off the lobes, stuff the inside with highly seasoned forcemeat no 417. Fasten it by means of a needle and coarse thread. Tie the heart up in paper and set it before a good fire being sure to keep it basted or it will eat dry as it has very little of its own fat. Two or three minutes before serving remove the paper, baste it well and service with good gravy or red currant jelly."

She noted "this is an excellent family dish, is very savoury and though not seen at many good tables may be recommended for its cheapness and economy."

As we shall see, cooking turtles was nearly as gruesome.

No one dared cook this Turtle

Illustration of Alice by Sir John Tenniel

Game

The Game's Afoot

After ordinary meat and poultry, Isabella devoted a long chapter to game. She introduced it with an essay on that favourite pastime of the British – hunting.

Thirty years after Isabella died, Oscar Wilde observed, when an English gentleman hunts the fox, the scene depicts "the unspeakable in pursuit of the uneatable."

But Isabella liked hunting. She started by explaining that the poets wrote about hunting from the start of poetry. "The themes which form the minstrelsy of the earliest ages either relate to the spoils of the chased or the dangers of the battlefield."

Love did not get a look in when it came to the start of poetry. Isabella pointed out that Nimrod "the first mighty hunter before the Lord" was introduced in the Bible. Ishmael became a good archer in "the solitudes of Arabia", while David was "not afraid of joining in combat with the lion or the bear", never mind sling shooting Goliath. The Greeks were also passionate about the hunt.

"Aristotle, sage as he was, advises young men to apply themselves to it; and Plato finds in it something divine."

The kings of England also loved hunting. And it didn't seem to matter if they were Saxon, Norman, Tudor or Windsor. Edward the Confessor, who didn't touch wine, women or song, could be turned on by hunting. "He took the greatest delight," Isabella quoted his chronicler, William of Malmesbury, "to follow a pack of swift hounds in pursuit of game". William the Conqueror and his sons took over the land that is now the New Forest so that they could hunt deer without being bothered by the Angles, Saxons or peasants. Edward III "was so enamoured of the exercise that he took with him sixty couples of stag hounds and every day amused himself with hawking or hunting."

George III does not seem to have been hunting mad but, then, he was really mad.

Vulture on toast

Hunting, Isabella said, contributed not only to "the promotion of health but for helping form that manliness of character which enters so largely into the composition of the sons of British toil."

Though she liked it, Isabella did admit that hunting could go to excess. She was harsh on the 1861 king of Naples. While he traveled to Vienna he killed "5 bears, 1820 boards, 1950 deer, 1145 does, 1625 roebucks, 11121 rabbits, 13 wolves, 17 badgers, 16354 hares and 354 foxes." And that was not the end of the destruction he caused en route. He also shot 15.350 pheasants and 12.335 partridges.

"Such an amount of destruction can hardly be called sport," Isabella thundered.

She quoted Soyer's *History of Food* where he points out that "some modern nations, the French among others, formerly ate the heron, crane, crow, stork, swan, cormorant and bittern." Another food writer, a certain Mr Belon, commented that "despite its revolting taste when unaccustomed to it the bittern is among the delicious treats of the French."

And the bittern was just an appetizer. Belon "also asserts that a falcon or vulture, either roasted or boiled, is excellent eating; and that if one of these birds happened to kill itself in flying after game, the falconer instantly cooked it."

Roast vulture – the perfect Sunday lunch.

Isabella added that "as the inevitable result of social progress is, at least to limit, if not to entirely suppress, such sports, much of the romance of country life has passed away." The decline of hunting and shooting everything that moved "may be less healthful and invigorating but certainly more elegant, intellectual and humanizing."

She went on to give advice on how to cook many species of game you rarely see at the butcher's now, like the black cock. She also had recipes for the landrail "which skulks in the thickest herbiage," the ptarmigan, the teal and the widgeon. "

Given the British passion for hunting, it's not surprising the landrail skulked in the thickest grass. To understand this passion, I want to quote from one of the great unsung heroes of Victorian Britain, Arthur Kavanagh. He was born with no arms and no legs in 1831 but his disability did not stop him becoming a crack shot – and in 1861, the year Isabella published her book – Arthur published *The Cruise of the Eva*. It was an account of hunting for pigs in Albania. Arthur always commented on The Bag.

In his book, Arthur explained that at first hunting in Albania did not go well. He and his party just did not decimate enough beasts. But then the night of February 22nd nearly made up for all the disappointments so far about the Bag. Arthur was sleeping on the brow of a hill when he heard "a tremendous crashing. Sleep vanished in a second." Excited, he cocked both barrels of his rifle and gazed intently into the bushes. In the dark it was not clear what animals were making the noise. He had "visions of a right and left with 2 mighty boars biting the dust". But when he could finally make out the beasts, they turned out to be a herd of cows on the rampage - and gentlemen did not shoot cows.

Arthur gave details at the end of the book of what they had managed to bring down in 20 days in Albania, his so-called Bag.

ARTHUR KAVANAGH'S BAG

Pigs 10	**Snipe 45**
Deer 6	**Plover 6**
Jackals 6	**Pigeons 24**
Geese 13	**Swan 1**
Duck 54	**Bittern 1**
Widgeon 152	**Sea Pheasant 7**
Teal 100	**Budgeter 3**
Woodcock 203	**Grebe Duck 4**

In his addiction to hunting, Kavanagh was typical of the Victorian gentleman.

ducks are not too beautiful to shoot

The Duck

Naturalists counted nearly a hundred species of ducks, Isabella wrote. Some were magnificent creatures like the Buenos Ayres duck.

"One would as soon think of picking a Chinese teal for luncheon or a goldfish for breakfast as to consign the handsome Buenos Ayres duck to the spit."

don't duck the issues

But there was no reason for the duck gourmet to despair, as there were over 100 different species you could roast. Isabella favoured Aylesbury ducks. They were bred with great tenderness. " In Buckinghamshire the cottagers often kept ducks," she noted.

"Round the wall of the living room and even the bedroom are fixed rows of wooden boxes lined with hay and it is the business of the wife and children to nurse and comfort the feathered lodgers, to feed the little ducklings and to take the old ones out for an airing."

It was important to plump up the ducks so they would be scrumptious.

"Unless ducks are supplied with a liberal feed of solid corn or grain, morning and evening, their flesh will become flabby and insipid." Isabella warned that when ducks were cooped up inside, they should not be allowed to stay too long in the water, when they got to it, because "they will then become ill, their feathers get rough and looseness of the bowels ensue."

The perfect Aylesbury duck "should be plump, pure white with yellow feet and a flesh coloured beak."

And then it was ready to be roasted, stewed with peas or turnips or just hashed.

Isabella took another swipe at the French on the subject of ducks. She pitied one very popular breed, the Rouen duck. "In Normandy and Brittany these ducks greatly abound and their livers are almost as popular as the pate de foie gras of Strasburg. In order to bring the livers of the wretched duck to the fashionable and unnatural size, the same diabolical cruelty is resorted to as in the case of the Strasburg goose."

Isabella did not flinch from the details. "The poor birds are nailed by the feet to a board placed closed to a fire and in that position are plentifully supplied with food and water. In a few days the carcass is reduced to a mere shadow while the liver has grown monstrously. We would rather abstain from the acquaintance of a man who ate pate de foie gras knowing its component parts."

Hunting in Greenland

The Grouse

These are divided into wood grouse, black grouse, red grouse, white grouse, Isabella noted. They are so unused to the sight of man "that they are easily shot and even snared."

It was related to the ptarmigan which was especially delicate. The naturalist Buffon said that the ptarmigan hated the heat and it could even be found in Greenland.

"It is esteemed delicious eating and its plumage is extremely beautiful."

There was even a species of grouse which had been over hunted. The Capercailzie had been known to be in Scotland but was extinct there now. It had last been seen in 1769 in the woods of Strathglass but now you had to go to Russia, Norway, the Alps or Siberia to find it.

Isabella recommended roast grouse, grouse pie which was made with rump steak and grouse salad.

A brave bird

The partridge

"This is a timorous bird, easily taken."

If so, Isabella did not explain how its character had changed over time because she also wrote;

> **"The Athenians trained this bird for fighting**
> **and Severus used to lighten the cares of**
> **royalty by witnessing the spirit of its combat.**
> **The Greeks esteemed its leg most highly"**
> **and refused to eat other parts of it.**
>
> **"The Romans ventured a little further**
> **and ate the breast while we consider**
> **the bird as wholly palatable.**
> **On account of the geniality of the**
> **climate it abounds most in the Ukraine."**

Isabella was struck by the fact that the partridge defended its young "in a remarkable manner." She quoted a famous but unnamed writer who reported "an extraordinary instance of an old bird's solicitude to save its brood".

But, alas, she did not tell us how the brave partridge defended her young.

Killing time

The Pheasant

"This beautiful bird is said to have been discovered by the Argonauts on the banks of the Phasis near Mount Ararat," Isabella noted.

Her recipes included roast pheasant, pheasant cutlets and an exotic one that she attributed to Brillat Savarin. It was called pheasant Sainte Alliance and the alliance was between pheasant and snipe. The pheasant should be stuffed with two snipe, with truffles, with beef lard and with an anchovy or two. It should be served up surrounded by Florida oranges.

"Do not be uneasy," Brillat Savarin said perhaps because your plebeian diner might wonder why Florida oranges, "about your dinner for a pheasant served in this way is fit for beings better than men."

To be worthy of being so stuffed, the pheasant had to be cooked just at the right moment, just before it started to go bad. Here Isabella became philosophical.

"Things edible have their degrees of excellence under various circumstances; thus asparagus, capers, peas, and partridges are best when young. Perfection in others is only reached in maturity."

With the pheasant that was very much the case.

"If the latter bird is eaten within three days of being killed then it has no peculiarity of flavour. Kept however a proper length of time – and this can be ascertained by a slight change of colour, it becomes a highly flavoured dish occupying the middle ground between chicken and venison. It is difficult to define any exact time to hang a pheasant; but any one possessed of the instincts of gastronomical science can at once detect the right moment when a pheasant should be taken down, in the same way that a good cook knows whether a bird should be removed from the spit or have one or two turns more."

But the British climate did not make it easy to deal with pheasants, as " it is not often that pheasants possess that exquisite taste which is acquired only by long keeping as the damp of this climate prevents them being kept as long as they are in other climates."

Olympian pigeons

The Pigeon

Isabella was brought up on Epsom race course and, as a child, she caught pigeons before the 2.30 handicap. This unusual life experience made her something of an expert on pigeons, how to breed them and how to cook them. She devotes 7 pages to pigeons and glories in describing different breeds from the Pouter Pigeon to the Jacobin.

"Their flesh is accounted savoury, delicate and stimulating and the dark coloured birds are considered to have the highest flavour. Pigeons," she noted, were "in the greatest perfection from midsummer to Michaelmas."

Pigeons had history too. "When Greece was in its glory, carrier pigeons were used to convey to distant parts the names of the victors of Olympiads."

The keeping and breeding of pigeons was big business – and Isabella could give detailed advice on how to keep a proper pigeon house.

"As cleanliness in human habitations is of the first importance so it is in the pigeon house," she said, and "there is one point which must be inevitably observed. And that is that every pair of pigeons has two holes or rooms to nest in. Without it there will be no security but the constant prospect of confusion, breaking of eggs and destruction of the young."

There also had to be a strategy for defeating cats. "Strange cats will frequently depopulate a whole dovecote." But cats could be useful in keeping away rats and mice "who will suck the eggs". The answer was to paint the pigeon house white "which is a favourite colour with pigeons."

One of the many interesting aspects of Isabella's philosophy is that she believed in harmony with nature. Mackerel should not be over fished, calves should not be killed too young. But that did not mean she was squeamish. She gave detailed instructions on how to kill and pluck pigeons.

Her recipes included boiled, broiled, roast and stewed pigeons, as well as her beloved Epsom pigeon pie which could also be made with steak.

Deer – a licence to print money?

Venison

For Isabella, venison was not just tasty but historic.

"Far away in ages past our fathers loved the chase," Isabella noted.

And she could trace man's love of hunting to the Bible.

"It is usually imagined that when Isaac ordered his son Esau to go out with his weapons his quiver and his bow, it was venison that he desired."

And the Greeks, Medes and Persians also loved it. "Xenophon in his history said the Cyrus, King of the Persians, ordered venison should never be wanting at his repasts. And of the effeminate Greeks it was the delight."

The triumph of Christianity did not change matters. Isabella wrote the venison was also a dish that the not too abstemious monks loved because it was also "the delight of Friar Tuck." Isabella argued that love of venison was even responsible for Hamlet. If William Shakespeare had not been accused of deer stealing in Strafford, he would never have had to leave town. The chain of causality is clear.

Shakespeare is accused of stealing deer, has to leave Stratford to keep out of trouble. Shakespeare heads for town, in London he will not be able to poach deer because the city is deer-less as well as peer-less

To maintain his venison habit, he becomes first a player and then a playwright. And, before long, "the finest dramatist in history."

Isabella gave splendid illustrations of the different kinds of deer households could buy at the butchers. It was an interesting story. Some enterprising landowners had decided the British needed more than fallow and red deer for their tables. In January 1859, when Isabella was writing the book, Viscount Hill introduced a number of South African deer to Surrey. The flavour of this deer was "infinitely superior," and aristocrats, with a taste for making money, also liked the fact that the new breed provided mountains of meat. The first beast Hill killed "weighed a stupendous 1176 lbs."

Bad habits

The Earl of Ducie had bred Persian deer and "Lord Hastings had a herd of Canadian wapiti, as well as Indian nyglkahgas and a small Indian hog deer."

But venison had to be just right. Isabella warned that "by running a sharp skewer into the meat close to the bone, its sweetness can be judged of."

After so much poetry in her description of the hunt and the different breeds, it is almost disappointing that she only offered 3 recipes – venison could be roasted, stewed or hashed.

Macbeth: *Will all great Neptune's ocean wash this venison Clean from my hand?*

Top ho turtle

Turtle Soup

Isabella included turtle among game. Sometimes Victorian cookery was really brutal. There is no better example of that than what an assiduous cook had to do to a turtle to make real – not mock – turtle soup.

"To make this soup with less difficulty cut off the head of the turtle the preceding day."

If the turtle was prepared the day before that "is generally preferable, the flavour being more uniform." Isabella did not tell her readers what to do with the decapitated turtle for 24 hours.

"In the morning, open the turtle by leaning heavily with a knife on the shell of the animals. Turn it upright on its end the flesh should be cut off along the spine with the knife sloping towards the bones for fear of touching the gall."

"Boil the back and the belly till the bones can be taken off."

The turtles came from the West Indies where they grazed "in submarine meadows and whence they are brought alive and in tolerable health."

Isabella noted that "this is the most expensive soup brought to the table as turtle is about 2 shillings a pound." It could also be bought tinned.

"The green turtle is highly prized on account of the delicious nature of its flesh, the fat of the upper and lower shields of the animal being esteemed the richest and most delicate parts. The soup, however, is likely to disagree with weak stomachs."

It was served sat the Lord Mayor's Banquet – and for others there was always mock turtle soup.

Rabbit, Rabbit, Rabbit

The rabbit shared one trait with the Cod. It could breed and breed and breed. Naturalists had observed it that "it breeds seven times a year and generally begets seven to eight young a time. If we suppose this to happen for a period of four years, the progeny that would spring from one pair would amount to more than a million."

This caused, Isabella noted, a crisis in the Balearic Islands during Roman times. "They (rabbits) infested the islands to such an extent that the inhabitants were obliged to implore the assistance of a military force from Augustus to exterminate them."

As with the pigeon, Isabella gave detailed advice on how to keep and breed the rabbits and on fancy rabbits. "Rabbits are divided into four kinds - warreners, parkers, hedgehogs and sweethearts. The warrener is a member of a subterranean community and is less effeminate than his kindred who dwell upon the earth and his fur is the most esteemed. After him comes the parker whose favourite resort is a gentleman's pleasure ground where he usually breeds in great numbers." Isabella didn't doubt her readers would know what a gentleman's pleasure ground was, but I am not sure contemporary readers will be quite so well-informed.

But the Victorians seemed willing to eat any kind of rabbit.

"The hedgehog is a sort of vagabond rabbit that, tinker like, roams about the country and would have a much better coat if he stayed at home. The sweetheart is a tame rabbit with its fur so soft, sleek and silky that it is also used in the important branch of hat making."

As usual, her pretty descriptions of the breeds of rabbit did not stop her being very matter of fact in giving advice.

"In purchasing this animal it ought to be remembered that both hares and rabbits when old have their claws ragged and blunt, their haunches thick and their ears dry and tough."

Ladies should not be fooled into buying any animal with such deficiencies.

"For boiling choose rabbits with smooth and sharp claws for that denotes that they are young,"

Fish

Loaves and Fishes

Isabella started her section on fish in Biblical vein. "The Jews are excellent cookers of fish," she pointed out, which reflected that humankind had been eating fish since Noah's Flood.

"As the NUTRITIVE PROPERTIES OF FISH (Isabella's capitals) are deemed inferior to those of what is called butcher's meat, it would appear, from all we can learn, that, in all ages, it has held only a secondary place in the estimation of those who have considered the science of gastronomy as a large element in the happiness of mankind. Among the Jews of old it was very little used, although it seems not to have been entirely interdicted, as Moses prohibited only the use of such as had neither scales nor fins."

In fact, it is kosher to eat most fish other than shellfish.

"The Egyptians, however, made fish an article of diet, notwithstanding that it was rejected by their priests. Egypt, however, is not a country favourable to the production of fish, although we read of the people, when hungry, eating it raw; of epicures among them having dried it in the sun; and of its being salted and preserved, to serve as a repast on days of great solemnity."

But it was definitely a dog eat dog world among the fish.

Isabella talks of the voracity of eels and of mackerels. And there were even dramas concerning the anchovy.

Victorians had an insatiable appetite for fish. According to figures from Mayhew's London poor, 1050,000,000 i.e 1050 million herrings were traded in London each year while the fish market also sold 4956, 896, 000 oysters.

These are very sobering statistics in the light of current anxieties about overfishing the sea.

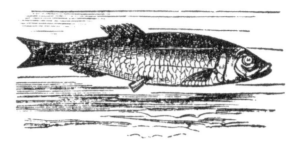

Herrings by the million

But Isabella felt that fish was not as nutritious as meat. And also while she enjoyed telling many myths that concerned beef and lamb, the sad fact was – and is – that fish, or at least the fish we eat, come with less mythology. After all, there are no recipes for mermaids.

It's also interesting that many kinds of fish that we now eat – shark, tuna, swordfish – were not available.

The Lobster Quadrille, Sir John Tenniel

Anchony fraud

Beware Fake Anchovies

"A general rule in choosing fish. A proof of freshness and goodness in most fishes is their being covered with scales – for if deficient in this respect it is a sign of their being stale or having been ill used."

"The anchovy was well known to the Greeks and Romans who prepared a liquor from it called garum which was held in great estimation.

The anchovy has been taken on the Hampshire Coast and in the British Channel. Other fish of inferior quality but resembling the real Gorgona anchovy are frequently sold for it and passed off as genuine"

Isabella was especially concerned by the quality of anchovy paste.

"Unfortunately in 6 cases out of 10, the only portion of these delicacies that contains anything of the anchovy is that paper label pasted on the bottle or pot on which the word Anchovy is printed. All the samples of anchovy paste analysed by different medical men have been found to be highly and vividly coloured with very large quantities of bole Armenian, The anchovy when taken is of a dark dead colour and it is to make it bright, handsome looking that this reed earth is used."

The rabbit of the seas

Cod

Isabella struck a very modern note when she wrote about cod, as she warned of the risks of what we call over-fishing.

"So extensive has been the consumption of this fish that it is surprising it did not long ago become extinct – which would certainly have been the case if it had not been for its wonderful powers of reproduction. So early as 1398, says Dr Cloquet, the inhabitants of Amsterdam had dispatched fishermen to the coasts of Sweden and in 1792, from the ports of France alone, 210 vessels went cod fishing."

Early Cod Wars

The French Revolution of 1789 had not done anything to stop the frogs getting their cod.

Isabella reckoned that 10000 boats were out fishing for cod in Europe alone. But it was not just nets the poor cods had to fear.

"If we add to this immense number the havoc made among the legions of cod by the larger scaly tribes of the great deep and take into account the destruction of the young by sea fowls and other inhabitants of the seas, besides the myriad of their eggs destroyed by accident, it becomes a miracle to find mighty multitudes of them still in existence. Yet it ceases to exercise our wonder when we remember that the female can every year give birth to more than 9,000,000 at a time."

It was all proof to Isabella "of the wise provision which Nature has made for the wants of man."

She gave good advice on how to pick the best fish. "Cod should be chosen for the table when it is plump and round near the tail where the hollow behind the head is deep and when the sides are undulated as if they were ribbed…The great point by which the cod should be judged is the firmness of its flesh. Although the cod is not firm when it is alive, the quality may be arrived at by pressing the finger into the flesh. If this rises immediately it is good; if not, it is stale."

She warned that sometimes cod who showed "signs of rough usage will eat much better than those with red gills," because all that had happened was the fish had been knocked about a bit when caught by the fishermen.

She offered many recipes for cod à la crème, curried cod, cod pie, cod sounds which were stuffed with oysters. In Newfoundland, which "is the favourite resort of the cod," the tongues were taken out and became a delicacy all of their own.

Crab and Prawn

Isabella noted that one particular species of crab, the black clawed was
by far the tastiest. Black clawed crabs were not specially rare as they were
found off the coast of Europe and of India. She only had two recipes for
crab but one was really exotic. It involved scraping out the crab meat and
serving it with a salamander.

Isabella's musings on crab allowed her to quote yet another poem by
Oppian who wrote of the hermit crab who literally eats another one out of
its shell.

**The hermit fish unarm'd by Nature left
Helpless and weak grow strong by harmless
theft
Fearful they stroll and look with panting wish
For the cast crust of some new cover'd fish.**

Eels

If we were not careful, eels would take over the world. They reproduced so easily and they tended to turn up in waters where they were not supposed to be. They also grew to an enormous size.

"They seldom come forth from their hiding places except in the night and in winter bury themselves deep in the mud on account of their susceptibility to the cold," Isabella winced.

The Eel Tribe

"Their aspect and manners approaches in some instances that of the serpent. They have a smooth head and slipper skin and are in general naked are covered with such small scales as are scarcely visible." They were also cunning and turned up "in waters where they had not been suspected."

Thus the mail'd tortoise and the wand'ring eel
Oft to the neighbouring beach will sometimes steal.

It is not simple to end the eel. "There is no fish so tenacious of life as this. After it is skinned and cut in pieces, the parts will continue to move for a considerable time, and no fish will live so long out of water."

The Voracity of the Eel

"We find in a note that Isaak Walton who wrote *The Compleat Angler* said that he knew eels, when kept in a pond, frequently destroyed ducks. From a canal near his house he missed many young ducks. And when the canal was drained, many eels were caught in the mud. When some of them were opened in their stomachs were found the undigested heads of the quacking tribe."

Forget duck à l'orange, the true delicacy was eel stuffed with duck!

Electric Eels

Isabella gave many recipes. Eels could be boiled and stewed and fried. They could be baked into a pie. But there are two extremely intriguing omissions in the book. First, jellied eels have been a favourite dish in London for centuries and Isabella never mentions them. Perhaps no middle class housewife would have such a working class dish in her house. Secondly, all good delicatessens now stock smoked eels as a delicacy. Again Isabella never records a recipe for them.

But what she does mention is Eel Broth in her section on invalid cookery. The bed bound Victorian could down "this very nutritious and easy of digestion."

If chicken soup cured all Jewish ills, eel broth apparently cured most Christian ones.

You can't be more dead than a dead herring

Forgotten Fish

Gudgeons, Gurnets and Herrings

Isabella recommended two fish that you hardly ever get now – the gudgeon and the gurnet.

The gudgeon had been one of the favourites in classical times. "It was highly esteemed in Greece and was, at the beginning of supper, served fried in Rome."

The gurnet or gurnard made Isabella remember Falstaff. "If I be not ashamed of my soldiers, I am a souced gurnet," the fat man recalled.

The herring had more history. And like the cod, the herring bred and bred.

"The herring tribe are found in the greatest abundance in the highest northern latitudes where they find a quiet retreat and security from their many enemies. Here they multiply beyond expression and in shoals come forth from their icy region to visit other portions of the great deep." The most effective of their enemies were, of course, the fishermen.

Isabella recommended baked and grilled herrings. She was also partial to herring roe which made "a nice relish by pounding it in a mortar with a little (not fake) anchovy."

The herring didn't last long once it has been caught. "The moment the herring is taken out of the water it dies. Hence the saying," Isabella noted, "dead as a herring." It's an expression that doesn't seem used any longer.

Left handed lobsters

The Lobster

In *Annie Hall,* there is a scene in which Woody Allen and Diane Keaton have to chase a lobster round the kitchen. But Keaton is far too tender-hearted to join in putting the lobster in boiling water so that it can be thermidor-ed. Isabella had no such scruples.

"Buy the lobsters alive and choose those that are heavy and full of motion because that is an indication of their freshness."

Making sure you got the lobster into the pot was not a sure thing because, Isabella noted in her aside on the Celerity of the Lobster, this was a super-speedy shell fish.It could run the 100 metres hurdles pretty fast.

"It could run even with the swiftness of a bird flying. Fishermen have seen some of them pass about 30 feet with a wonderful degree of swiftness."

But Isabella's own lobsters did not get the chance to run away. "Have ready a saucepan of boiling water, put in the lobster and keep it boiling for 20 minutes and do not forget to skim the water."

Though its eventual fate was to be boiled alive in Belgravia, the lobster also provided the perfect example of the dog eat dog life of the deep. When it cast off its shell, as it did every year, the lobster was in a pickle.

"Previously to the throwing off of its old shell, it appears sick, languid and restless but in the course of a few days, it is entirely invested in its new coat of armour. Whilst it is in a defenceless state though, it seeks some lonely place where it may lie undisturbed and escape the horrid fate of being devoured by one of its own species who have the advantage of still being encased in their mail."

Lobsters, Isabella wrote, have two rather different claws – one has nobs and one is serrated. "With the former it keeps firm hold of submarine plants and with the latter it cuts and minces food with great dexterity." But what was striking was that the "knobbed or numb claw, as fisherman sometimes call it, is sometimes on the left and sometimes on the right." In other words, some lobsters must be left handed.

The lost lobster

The psychology of the lobster was also interesting because, though it could run like a hound - well sort of - it liked nothing better than staying at home, according to an unnamed poet Isabella quoted.

Nothing like their home the constant lobster prize
And foreign shores and unknown seas despise
Though cruel hands the banish'd wretch expel
And force the captive from his native cell
He will, if freed, return with anxious care
Find the known rock and to his home repair
No novel customs learns in different seas
But wonted food and home taught manners please."

And if a lobster was afraid, it could root itself to a spot like a nimble goat.

Her recipes included Lobster cutlets, lobster patties, potted lobster, lobster salad, though not lobster thermidor.

gorgeous mackerel

The Mackerel

Isabella was poetic about this fish.

"This is not just one of the most elegantly formed but one of the most beautifully coloured fish when taken from the sea.

Death impairs the vivid splendors of its colours but it does not entirely obliterate them.

For a short time they exhibit a phosphoric glow".

Mackerel would be boiled, broiled, baked or pickled and that might be just what they deserved.

Murder by Mackerel

"The voracity of this fish is very great and from their immense numbers they are bold in attacking objects which they might otherwise be expected to dread. Pontoppidan tells of a sailor from a ship lying in one of the harbours of the coast of Norway who having gone into the sea to bathe was suddenly missed. Within a few minutes he was seen on the surface with great numbers of mackerel clinging to him by their mouths. His comrades hastened to his assistance. But when they had struck the fishes from him, and got him, they found he was so severely bitten, he shortly afterwards expired."

MACKEREL IN STICK UP DRAMA!

A Fishy Tale

The lurking scallop

Oysters

Isabella wanted to clear up one confusion. Some misguided naturalist had said that "oysters and scallops belong to one tribe." This was because they were both hinged. But the naturalist was unhinged, she suggested.

"Oysters usually adhere to rocks, or one or two species, to the roots of trees on the shore while scallops are always detached and usually lurk in the sand."

Today most cookbooks would cover the aphrodisiac qualities of the oyster. Isabella did not offer any clue to that but she did note one oyster excess of the 18th century. She quoted one of her favourite sources, Brillat Savarin's *The Physiology of Taste*. He noted that at the end of the 18th century "it was common for well arranged entertainment in Paris to start with oysters and that many guests were not contented without swallowing twelve dozen." Brillat Savarin calculated that 108 oyster eater would have eaten about 3 lbs of oysters flesh. Even if you were a champion glutton, you would be very full if you had eaten so much chicken or fish.

But oysters were lighter so greedy guts could consume them as if they were peanuts. Brillat Savarin told the story of one of his dinner companions who downed 32 dozen oysters before the main course.

The oyster fishery was so important that it was regulated by the Court of the Admiralty. There were strict seasons when fishermen could take oysters. After May "it is punishable to take any oyster between the shells of which a shilling will rattle."

Isabella had an interesting method of keeping oysters.

"Put them in a tub and cover them with salt and water. Let them remain for 12 hours when they are to be taken out and allowed to stand another 12 hours without water."

The best oysters in Britain came from Essex and Suffolk She noted that the best oysters had a green tinge. Her recipes were for fried oysters, oysters patties, and raw oysters.

The psychopathic pike

Perch, Pike.

Today, while we regularly eat some fish Isabella never mentioned, specialist fishmongers hardly exist. Supermarkets usually stock cod, haddock, salmon, mackerel, sole, trout, tuna and perhaps swordfish. Isabella's readers had far more fresh water fish to choose from, just as they had more diverse game. Isabella offered recipes for pike, perch, carp and sprats.

She recommended perch stewed with wine and made some interesting observation on the pike;

"This fish is, on account of its voracity, termed the fresh water shark". She mentioned that there were some smaller lakes in Ireland which had been a favourite place for trout. And then the pikes arrived and "the trout becomes extinct."

But she found one poem which suggested the pike was not quite such a psychopath.

> **The pike, fell tyrant of the liquid plain,**
> **With ravenous waste devours his fellow train**
> **Yet howso'er with raging famine pined**
> **The tench he spares, a medicinal kind;**
> **For when by wounds distressed, or sore disease,**
> **He courts the salutary fish for ease;**
> **Close to his scales the kind physician glides**
> **And sweats a healing balsam from his sides."**

Acidly, Isabella added; "in our estimation this self denial in the pike may be attributed to a less poetical cause" – and that was the "mud loving disposition of the tench. It keeps itself so completely concealed at the bottom of its aqueous haunts that it remains secure from the attacks of its predatory neighbour."

Perch and pike had to be done simply boiled or baked though she did give one recipe for perch stewed in wine.

Painting the salmon red

The Salmon

"This is the abdominal fish", Isabella said. She then quoted Isaak Walton, the author of *The Compleat Angler* who called the salmon - "the king of fresh water fish." Unlike kingly beef, she had few myths and legends about salmon to tell so she concentrated on its natural history.

She had firm advice on how to choose a decent salmon. "The belly should be firm and thick which may be readily ascertained by feeling it with finger and thumb." And, as ever, she warned against dodgy purveyors. They had managed to convince many writers on cookery that if a salmon had red gills it was excellent. But "this is not to be relied on as this quality can easily be given by art." Obviously Victorian fish mongers kept a paint brush at the back of the shop and were all too apt to dab a touch of red on the fish to make it look good.

By 1860, it was known that salmon were cold water fish. They were found on the borders of Siberia in the Kamschatka Peninsula, but they had never been caught in the Mediterranean. This made one plan very ambitious. "In 1859 great efforts were made to introduce this fish into the Australian colonies, "Isabella noted. At first they failed, but the heroic culture that had built railways across deserts was not going to be defeated by fish. Isabella reported "it is believed that after many difficulties which were very skillfully overcome, it was very successful."

She was intrigued by the fact that the salmon returned to its native river to spawn. She wrote; "this is one of the most curious circumstances in natural history. As the swallow returns annually to its nest so it (the salmon) returns to the same spot to deposit its ova. The fact seems to have been repeatedly proved."

And the salmon was also an explorer, which had been used recently in scientific experiments.

"Dr Bloch states that gold and silver rings have been attached to the same salmon to prove a communication existed between the Northern and Caspian seas and that the experiment succeeded."

The Soul of the Sole

"The salmon is said to be averse to anything red," she noted so salmon fishermen wore different coloured smocks.

Isabella had more recipes for salmon than for any other fish. It could be curried, collared, crimped, served as cutlets, pickled, cured and potted. Today smoked salmon is common, but it is never mentioned in the book.

The Sole

This ranked next to the turbot in point of excellence among flat fish, Isabella said.

They were not that easy to catch because they were so flat.

The finest are caught in Torbay and frequently weigh 8lbs to 10 lbs per pair.

Her recipes included fried soles, Sole with cream pie boiled soles.

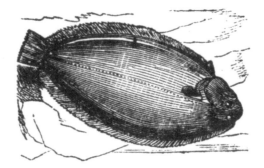

Sprats

Isabella also liked small fish such as sprats but here, as in dealing with the turtle, we see her no nonsense approach or brutal approach. There was no room in her kitchen for the squeamish.

"Sprats should be cooked very fresh which can be ascertained by their bright and sparkling eyes. Wipe them dry, fasten them in rows by a skewer run through their eyes."

Turbot

The London market was chiefly supplied by Dutch fishermen who bring 90000 head to it, Isabella said.

"The flesh is firm and gelatinous and the better for being kept a day or two before cooking it."

The turbot meant something to the ancient Romans, she said;

"As this luxurious people compared soles to partridges and sturgeons to peacock they found a resemblance between the turbot and the pheasant."

Once in the Emperor's Domitian's time, "it is said that one sole was taken of such proportions as to require in the imperial kitchen a new stove to be erected, for not even imperial Rome could furnish a stove or dish large enough for the monstrous animal."

She recommended an interesting way of dressing turbot. "Take the crumbs out of a stale loaf, cut it into small pyramids, put rather more than a tablespoon of white of eggs beaten to a stiff froth. Over this sprinkle finely chopped parsley and fine raspings of a dark colour." It would look very pretty.

Her recipes included baked fillets of turbot, turbot à la crème, boiled turbot, turbot with cheese and turbot à l'italienne which the Romans had loved.

1. Boiled Turbot.　2. Dressed Crab.　3. Boiled Salmon Trout.

Sauces and Pickles

Madam, where is your pickle?

On sauces, Pickles and Dressings

"The ancient Roman and Greeks held their pickles in high estimation. Their cooks prepared pickles with the greatest care."

As the Victorians did not have refrigeration, pickling was very important for it allowed many foodstuffs to be kept for a long period of time. And it was vital to be able to produce the right pickle fast.

"Nothing shows more the difference between a tidy and thrifty housewife and a lady to whom these desirable epithets could not be applied honestly than the appearance of their respective store cupboards."

The Competent Housewife "is able at any moment to put her hand on any condiment at once. No dish should be spoilt for the want a little soothing."

The Untidy Housewife, however, "hunts all over the cupboard for the ketchup the cook requires or the pickle the husband thinks he should like a little of with his cold mutton chop or roast beef."

Isabella advised the slovenly housewife who could never locate her Mushroom Ketchup that if she wanted to get into good Society, she had better put all her pickles in order.

Otherwise the servants might well start whispering.

Given the importance of pickles, Isabella gave advice on how pickle lemons, (with and without peel) nasturtiums, beetroots, onions, red cabbage, walnuts, cucumbers, capsicums, mushrooms. She even had a recipe for the pickle to end - or encompass - all pickles.

Universal Pickle

"As this pickle takes 2 to 3 months to make care must be taken to keep the jar which contains the pickle well covered either with a closely fitting lid or with a piece of bladder securely tied over."

Grotesque sauces

Sauces and Gravies in the Middle Ages

Neither poultry, butcher's meat nor roast game were eaten dry in the Middle Ages. Different sauces, each with their own peculiar flavour, were served with all these dishes.

.

Strange and grotesque sauces such as "butter fried and roasted were invented by the cooks of those days. But these preparations had hardly any merit other than of being surprising and difficult to make."

It makes one wonder what she would have thought of our contemporary fad for bacon and eggs ice cream.

Isabella went on to praise the modern housewife – a phrase she often used – who could turn out a dinner party fast.

"But talking of speed and time and preparation, "Isabella said, " what a combination of all these must have been necessary for the feast at the wedding of Charles VI of France. The chronicler Froissart (who is best known for his account of the Crusades) tells us that the art of cooking with its paraphernalia of sauces, with gravy, cinnamon, pepper, garlic, scullion, brains, gravy soup, milk potage and ragouts had a signal place. The skilful chef covered the marble table of the palace with no less than a hundred different dishes prepared in a hundred different ways."

Isabella noted that Louis XII of France granted a monopoly to a company of sauce makers. If anyone else stirred a Hollandaise or Bearnaise, they'd be stuck in jail. "The statutes drawn up by this company inform us that the famous sauce à la cemeline was to be composed of good ginger, good cinnamon, good cloves, good grains of paradise and good vinegar. May we respectfully express a hope – not that we desire to doubt it in the least – that the English sauce manufacturers of the 19th century are equally considerate and careful in choosing their ingredients for their well known sauces."

I've not been able to find a grain of paradise yet, but it sounds good!

Mrs custard invents mustard

Mustard

Isabella clearly liked her mustard. She said;

"It is the best stimulant to impart strength to the digestive organs."

Diligent as ever, she managed to unearth an interesting piece of mustard history.

"Before 1720 mustard was not known at English tables. Then an old woman by the name of Clements began to grind the seed in a mill and to pass the flour through the several processes necessary to free the seed from the husks. She kept her secret for many years during which she sold large quantities of mustard throughout the country but especially to London. Here it was introduced to the royal table where it met the approval of George I."
(Yes her name was Clements not Custard before aggrieved Aga-niks start complaining but still!)

The British navy ran on rum, the lash and sodomy, Winston Churchill said – and he had been First Sea Lord.

But the Roman army, Isabella revealed, ran on vinegar. It was the wonder-drink of the legions.

Vinegar

"Nearly all ancient nations were acquainted with the use of vinegar. We learn in Ruth that the reapers of the East soaked their bread in it to freshen it. The Romans kept large quantities of it in their cellar. This people attributed very beneficial qualities to it. It was supposed to be digestive, antibilious and antiscrobutic. Spartanius (a Roman historian) tells us that Roman soldiers relied on their vinegar to brave the inclemency and different climates of Europe."

She added that the Spanish labourers refreshed themselves with vinegar. And even in foggy Britain, vinegar had its appeal. Isabella offered many recipes for different kinds of vinegar, including making it out of chilies, cucumbers, gooseberries, raspberries and mint.

Thus Spoke Julius Caesar

I came...

I saw...

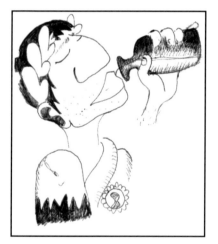

I drank vinegar.

I got indegestion.

The best fats

Under Sauces, Isabella also included sections on fats. She had no reservations about butter which we now fret clogs our arteries.

Butter

"About the second century of the Christian era butter was placed by Galen in amongst the useful medical agents," Isabella said.

"Dioscorides mentioned that he had noticed that fresh butter was served at meals instead of oil and that it took the place of fat in making pastry. Thus we have undoubted authority that 1800 years ago there existed a knowledge of the useful qualities of butter. The Romans seem to have set about making it much as we do. Pliny tells us 'Butter is made from milk and the use of this aliment so much thought after by the barbarian nations, distinguishes the rich from the common people."

Isabella quotes Soyer's *History of Food* which says that "to obtain butter instantly it is only necessary in summer to put new milk into a bottle some hours after it has been taken from a cow and shake it briskly. The clots which are then formed should be thrown into a sieve, washed and pressed together and they constitute the finest and most delicate butter than can possibly be made."

Rancid butter should be melted several times and well kneaded.

The other favourite fats of the Victorians were lard for which she followed a recipe by Soyer.

And our current healthy favourite

Olive oil

Isabella noted that there was an olive branch in the mouth of the dove that returned to Noah's ark and spoke of the Mount of Olives. Winner of the events at the Greek Olympics were decorated with olive leaves. At the time olive oil came from France, Spain and Italy. Oil extracted from Lucca was best.

And fats brought Isabella to what was dear to her heart – the galaxy of puddings the Victorians loved to eat.

Puddings

On Puddings

Puddings brought out the poet in Isabella. She introduced this section with a history of cereals since she reckoned you could not have puddings without cereal. As history showed

"Here is the recipe for the ancient Athenian national dish, the barley gruel of the gladiators and the common people was much the same." Isabella gave a Roman recipe in which red wheat flour was put in a bowl. It was then cooked with three pounds of cream cheese, half a pound of honey and one egg. She noted that;

"Scrupulous attention should be paid to the cleanliness of pudding clothes as from neglect in this particular, the outsides of boiled puddings often taste very disagreeable indeed."

Isabella offers recipes for an astonishing variety of puddings including Aunt Nell's Pudding, baked apple, boiled apple, creamed apple tarts, bachelor's pudding which was made of grated bread, currants and essence of lemon, baroness pudding whose recipe was given to Isabella by a baroness who insisted the key was

boil

boil

and boil it.

A Galaxy of Puddings

As Isabella said, "this pudding the editress cannot recommend too highly." I have listed it among her top 40 recipes.

There were equally many varieties of bread pudding including miniature bread pudding, canary pudding – which did not have any canary in it. Sadly Isabella did not explain why it got its name. She continued her pudding rhapsody with Delhi Pudding, Empress Pudding, Exeter Pudding which was very rich as it included dollops of cream, German Pudding, Golden Pudding and Herodotus Pudding. Herodotus was a Greek historian and the pudding got its name because it used figs which grew in Greece.

There many lemon puddings and more jellies than one can imagine. Then she came to Mansfield Pudding and Military Puddings.

Under P she explained how to make *Puits d'Amour* which means literally Wells of Love. Paradise Pudding, Plum Pudding and Potato Pudding followed.

Isabella then offered ten recipes for different kinds of rice pudding.

She also favoured Quickly Made Pudding, Vicarage Pudding, a Vol au Vent of Strawberries with Whipped Cream, West Indian Pudding and Everton Pudding.

But this galaxy of puddings did not include what many people today think of as the best of all dessert ingredients.

The origins of chocolate

Chocolate

Today whole books are devoted to chocolate, so it is surprising to find that Isabella has only 5 entries about it. She worried that readers would imagine chocolate came from the cocoa-nut tree.

"The tree from which chocolate is procured is very different – the Theobroma cocoa. The cocoa trees was cultivated by the aboriginal inhabitants of South America particularly in Mexico where, according to Humboldt, (the author of a standard work on the Conquest of Mexico) it was reared by Montezuma. It was transplanted into other dependencies of the Spanish monarchy in 1520; and it was so highly esteemed by Linnaeus as to receive the name of Theobroma, a term derived from the Greeks and signifying food for the gods."

It was a great luxury because the government imposed such high duties on it. But then the tax on chocolates was reduced. Even though many households could now afford it, Isabella only included two recipes which used it ~ Chocolate Soufflé and ~ Chocolate Cream.

Her other mention of it is that she notes a box of chocolates - "This is served in an ornamental box" – is a nice gift and one that the elegant housewife can display on the tazza.

What she would have made of our chocolate fetish?

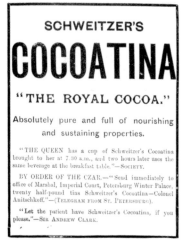

Oranges, lemons and grapes

A dish of fruit

Isabella recommended that a dinner party should end with the guests picking at a nice dish of fruit. And she had ideas on how these should be presented.

"By putting a layer of moss, so much fruit is not required. Grapes should be placed on top of the fruit, a portion of the bunches hanging over the sides of the dish in a negligee kind of manner."

One fruit made the dish seem grand and sophisticated.

"France produces about a thousand varieties of grape. Hygienists agree in pronouncing the grape among the best of fruits. The grape possesses several rare qualities. It is nourishing and fattening and its prolonged use has often overcome the most obstinate cases of constipation."

The skin and the pips, she warned, should not be eaten because they could be hard on the delicate digestive system of her readers.

Before coming to Isabella's top 40 recipes, I can't help noticing the many differences between the cooking she recommended and cooking today. Though Isabella was more than a little in love with French cooking and advocated more use of such then exotic ingredients as macaroni, she hardly mentioned foods that are very common now.

There is no charcuterie in the book. There is no mention of Chinese food and, despite the fact that Queen Victoria ruled India, there is virtually no mention of Indian food. There are only a few mentions of curry which replaced roast beef as Britain's favourite dish sometime in the 1990s.

And while Isabella worried about the health of her readers, there is no talk of dieting. The Victorians loved, loved, loved food!.

I will return to the question of what we can learn from Isabella at the end of the book.

DISH OF APPLES.

DISH OF MIXED SUMMER FRUIT.

ALMONDS AND RAISINS.

DISH OF STRAWBERRIES.

Mrs. Beeton's Top 40

Soup à la Cantatrice

(An Excellent Soup, very Beneficial for the Voice.)

119. INGREDIENTS. – 3 oz. of sago, ½ pint of cream, the yolks of 3 eggs, 1 lump of sugar, and seasoning to taste, 1 bay-leaf (if liked), 2 quarts of medium stock No. 105

Mode – Having washed the sago in boiling water, let it be gradually added to the nearly boiling stock. Simmer for ½ an hour, when it should be well dissolved. Beat up the yolks of the eggs, add to them the boiling cream; stir these quickly in the soup, and serve immediately. Do not let the soup boil, or the eggs will curdle.

Time. – 40 minutes. Average cost, 1s. 6d. per quart.

Seasonable all the year. Sufficient for 8 persons.

At today's prices this would cost
Cream £1
3 eggs 40p
Stock 15p

Around £2 per quart

Vegetable Soup

Good and cheap, made without meat

161. INGREDIENTS. – 6 potatoes, 4 turnips, or 2 if very large; 2 carrots, 2 onions; if obtainable, 2 mushrooms; 1 head of celery, 1 large slice of bread, 1 small saltspoonful of salt, ¼ saltspoonful of ground black pepper, 2 teaspoonfuls of Harvey's sauce, 6 quarts of water.

Mode. – Peel the vegetables, and cut them up into small pieces; toast the bread rather brown, and put all into a stewpan with the water and seasoning. Simmer gently for 3 hours, or until all is reduced to a pulp, and pass it through a sieve in the same way as pea-soup, which it should resemble in consistence; but it should be a dark brown colour. Warm it up again when required; put in the Harvey's sauce, and, if necessary, add to the flavouring.

Time. – 3 hours, or rather more. Average cost, 1d. per quart.

Seasonable at any time. Sufficient for 16 persons.

At today's prices this would cost;

Celery 75p
Mushroom 15p
Turnips 30p
Potatoes 50p
Carrots 20p

Total £2

A Good Mutton Soup

175. INGREDIENTS. – A neck of mutton about 5 or 6 lbs., 3 carrots, 3 turnips, 2 onions, a large bunch of sweet herbs, including parsley; salt and pepper to taste; a little sherry, if liked; 3 quarts of water.

Mode. – Lay the ingredients in a covered pan before the fire, and let them remain there the whole day, stirring occasionally. The next day put the whole into a stewpan, and place it on a brisk fire. When it commences to boil, take the pan off the fire, and put it on one side to simmer until the meat is done. When ready for use, take out the meat, dish it up with carrots and turnips, and send it to table; strain the soup, let it cool, skim off all the fat, season and thicken it with a tablespoonful, or rather more, of arrowroot; flavour with a little sherry, simmer for 5 minutes, and serve.

Time.- 15 hours. Average cost, including the meat, 1s. 3d. per quart.

Seasonable at any time. Sufficient for 8 persons.

At today's prices this would cost;

Mutton £3
Carrots 20p
Turnips 20p
Onions 20p
Sherry 40p

Total £4

Indian Pickle

(very Superior)

451. INGREDIENTS.- To each gallon of vinegar allow 6 cloves of garlic, 12 shallots, 2 sticks of sliced horseradish, ¼ lb. of bruised, ginger, 2 oz of whole black pepper, 1 oz of long pepper, 1 oz of allspice, 12 cloves, ¼ oz of cayenne, 2 oz of mustard-seed, ¼ lb of mustard, 1 oz of turmeric; a white cabbage, cauliflowers, radishpods, French beans, gherkins, small round pickling-onions, nasturtiums, caspsicums, chilies, &c.

Mode.-Cut the cabbage, which must be hard and white, into slices, and the cauliflowers into small branches; sprinkle salt over them in a large dish, and let them remain two days; dry them, and put them into a very large jar, with garlic, shallots, horseradish, ginger, pepper, allspice, and cloves, in the above proportions. Boil sufficient vinegar to cover them, which pour over, and, when cold, cover up to keep them free from dust. As the other things for the pickle ripen at different times, they may be added as they are ready: these will be radish-pods, French beans, gherkins, small onions, nasturtiums, capsicums, chilies, &c. &c. As these are procured, they must, first of all, be washed in a little cold vinegar, wiped, and then simply added to other ingredients in the large jar, only taking care that they are covered by the vinegar. If more vinegar should be wanted to add to the pickle, do not omit first to boil it before adding it to the rest.

When you have collected all the things you require, turn all out in a large pan, and thoroughly mix them. Now put the mixed vegetables into smaller jars, without any of the vinegar; then boil the vinegar again, adding as much more as will be required to fill the different jars, and cayenne, mustard-seed, turmeric, and mustard, which must be well mixed with a little cold vinegar, allowing the quantities named above to each gallon of vinegar. Pour the vinegar, boiling hot, over the pickle, and when cold, tie down with a bladder. If the pickle is wanted for immediate use, the vinegar should be boiled twice more, but the better way is to make it during one season for use during the next. It will keep for years, if care is taken that the vegetables are quite covered by the vinegar.

This recipe was taken from the directions of a lady whose pickle was always pronounced excellent by all who tasted it, and who has, for many years, exactly followed the recipe given above.

Leamington Sauce

(an Excellent Sauce for Flavouring Gravies, Hashes, Soups, &c).

459. INGREDIENTS.- Walnuts. To each quart of walnut-juice allow 3 quarts of vinegar, 1 pint of Indian soy, 1 oz of cayenne, 2 oz of shallots, ¾ oz of garlic, ½ pint of port wine.

Mode.- Be very particular in choosing the walnuts as soon as they appear in the market; for they are more easily bruised before they become hard and shelled. Pound them in a mortar to a pulp, strew some salt over them, and let them remain thus for two or three days, occasionally stirring and moving them about. Press out the juice, and to each quart of walnut-liquor allow the above proportion of vinegar, soy, cayenne, shallots, garlic, and port wine. Pound each ingredient separately in a mortar, then mix them well together, and store away for use in small bottles. The corks should be well sealed.

Seasonable.- This sauce should be made as soon as walnuts are obtainable, from the beginning to the middle of July.

Mixed Pickle

(Very Good).

471. INGREDIENTS.- To each gallon of vinegar allow $\frac{1}{4}$ lb. of bruised ginger, $\frac{1}{4}$ lb of mustard, $\frac{1}{4}$ lb of salt, 2oz of mustard-seed, 1 oz of turmeric, 1oz of ground black pepper, $\frac{1}{4}$ oz, of cayenne, cauliflowers, onions, celery, sliced cucumbers, gherkins, French beans, nasturtiums, capiscums.

Mode.- Have a large jar, with a tightly-fitting lid, in which put as much vinegar as required, reserving a little to mix the various powders to a smooth paste. Put into a basin the mustard, tumeric, pepper and cayenne; mix them with vinegar, and stir well until no lumps remain; add all the ingredients to the vinegar, and mix well. Keep in a warm place, and thoroughly stir every morning for a month with a wooden spoon, when it will be ready for different vegetables to be added to it. As these come into season, have them gathered on a dry day, and , after merely wiping them with a cloth, to free them from moisture, put them into the pickle. The cauliflowers, it may be said, must be divided into small bunches. Put all these into the pickle raw, and at the end of the season, when there have been added as many of the vegetables as could be procured, store it away in jars, and tie over with bladder. As none of the ingredients are boiled, this pickle will not be fit to eat till 12 months have elapsed. Whilst the pickle is being made, keep a wooden spoon tied to the jar; and its contents, it may be repeated, must be stirred every morning.

Seasonable.-Make the pickle liquor in May or June, as the season arrives for the various vegetables to be picked.

Pickled Onions

(a very Simple Method, and exceedingly Good).

486. INGREDIENTS.-Pickling onions; to each quart of vinegar, 2 teaspoonfuls of allspice, 2 teaspoonfuls of whole black pepper.

Mode.- Have the onions gathered when quite dry and ripe, and, with the fingers, take off the thin outside skin; then, with a silver knife (steel should not be used, as it spoils the colour of the onions), remove one more skin, when the onion will look quite clear. Have ready some very dry bottles or jars, and as fast as they are peeled, put them in. Pour over sufficient cold vinegar to cover them, with pepper and allspice in the above proportions, taking care that each jar has its share of the latter ingredients. Tie down with bladder, and put them in a dry place, and in a fortnight they will be fit for use. This is a most simple recipe and very delicious, the onions being nice and crisp. They should be eaten within 6 or 8 months after being done, as the onions are liable to become soft.

Seasonable from the middle of July to the end of August.

Salad Dressing

(Excellent)

506. INGREDIENTS.- 1 teaspoonful of mixed mustard, 1 teaspoonful of pounded sugar, 2 tablespoonfuls of salad oil, 4 tablespoonfuls of milk, 2 tablespoonfuls of vinegar, cayenne and salt to taste.

Mode.-Put the mixed mustard into a salad-bowl with the sugar, and add the oil drop by drop, carefully stirring and mixing all these ingredients well together. Proceed in this manner with milk and vinegar, which must be added very gradually, or the sauce will curdle. Put in the seasoning, when the mixture will be ready for use. If this dressing is properly made, it will have a soft creamy appearance, and will be found very delicious with crab, or cold fried fish (the latter cut into dice), as well as with salads. In mixing salad dressings, the ingredients cannot be added too gradually, or stirred too much.

Average cost, for this quantity, 3d, or roughly 50p in today's money.

Sufficient for a small salad. This recipe can be confidently recommended by the editress, to whom it was given by an intimate friend noted for her salads.

Tomato Sauce for Keeping

(Excellent).

530. INGREDIENTS.- To every quart of tomato-pulp allow 1 pint of cayenne vinegar (NO. 386), ¾ oz. of shallots, ¾ oz. of garlic, peeled and cut in slices; salt to taste. To every six quarts of liquor, 1 pint of soy, 1 pint of anchovy sauce.

Mode.-Gather the tomatoes quite ripe; bake them in a slow oven till tender; rub them through a sieve, and to every quart of pulp add cayenne vinegar, shallots, garlic, and salt, in the above proportion; boil the whole together till the garlic and shallots are quite soft; then rub it through a sieve, put it again into a saucepan, and, to every six quarts of the liquor, add 1 pint of soy and the same quantity of anchovy sauce, and boil together for about 20 minutes; bottle off for use, and carefully seal or rosin the corks. This will keep good for 2 or 3 years, but will be fit for use in a week. A useful and less expensive sauce may be made by omitting the anchovy and soy.

Seasonable.-Make this from the middle of September to the end of October.

PICKLED WALNUTS

(Very Good).

534. INGREDIENTS.-100 walnuts, salt and water. To each quart of vinegar allow 2 oz. of black pepper, 1 oz. of allspice, 1oz. of bruised ginger.

Mode.-Procure the walnuts while young; Place the walnuts in salted water, 4lbs of salt to each gallon of water, letting them remain 9 days, and changing the brine every third day; drain them off, put them on a dish, place it in the sun until they become perfectly black, which will be in 2 or 3 days; have ready dry jars, into which place the walnuts, and do not quite fill the jars. Boil sufficient vinegar to cover them, for 10 minutes, with spices in the above proportion, and pour it hot over the walnuts, which must be quite covered with the pickle; tie down with bladder, and keep in a dry place. They will be fit for use in a month, and will keep good 2 or 3 years.

Time.- 10 minutes.

Seasonable.- Make this from the beginning to the middle of July, before the walnuts harden.

White Sauce

(Good).

537. INGREDIENTS.- ½ pint of white stock (no.107), ½ pint of cream, 1 dessertspoonful of flour, salt to taste.

Mode.- Have ready a delicately-clean saucepan, into which put the stock, which should be well flavoured with vegetables, and rather savoury; mix the flour smoothly with the cream, add it to the stock, season with a little salt, and boil all these ingredients very gently for about 10 months, keeping them well stirred the whole time, as this sauce is very liable to burn.

Time.- 10 minutes.

Average cost, 1s.

Sufficient for a pair of fowls. Seasonable at any time.

Today's cost

Cream £0.70 p
Stock cube 10 p
Total 80p

Rolled Loin of Mutton

(Very Excellent)

729. INGREDIENTS – About 6lbs of a loin of mutton, ½ teaspoonful of pepper, ¼ teaspoonful of pounded allspice, ¼ teaspoonful of mace, ¼ teaspoonful of nutmeg, 6 cloves, forcemeat No 417, 1 glass of port wine, 2 tablespoonfuls of mushroom ketchup.

Mode- Hang the mutton till tender, bone it, and sprinkle over it pepper, mace, cloves, allspice, and nutmeg in the above proportion, all of which must be pounded very fine. Let it remain for a day, then make a forcemeat by recipe No. 417, cover the meat with it, and roll and bind it up firmly. Half bake it in a slow oven, let it grow cold, take off the fat, and put the gravy into a stewpan; flour the meat, put it in the gravy, and stew it till perfectly tender. Now take out the meat, unbind it, add to the gravy wine and ketchup as above, give one boil, and pour over the meat. Serve with red-current jelly; and, if obtainable, a few mushrooms stewed for a few minutes in the gravy, will be found a great improvement.

Time – 1 ½ hour to bake the meat, 1 ½ hour to stew gently.

Average cost, 4s 9d.

Sufficient for 5 or 6 persons.

Today's cost would be about £6

Seasonable at any time.

Note – This joint will be found very nice if rolled and stuffed, as here directed, and plainly roasted. It should be well basted, and served with a good gravy and currant jelly.

Royalists should note Prince Charles recently made a plea for us to re-discover the joys of mutton.

Minced Veal, with Bechamel Sauce (Cold Meat Cookery)

(Very Good)

889. INGREDIENTS-The remains of a fillet of veal, 1 pint of Bechamel sauce No. 367, ½ teaspoonful of minced lemon peel, forcemeat balls.

Mode – Cut- but do not chop- a few slices of cold roast veal as finely as possible, sufficient to make rather more than 1 lb, weighed after being minced. Make the above proportion of Bechamel, by recipe NO 367; add the lemon-peel, put in the veal, and let the whole gradually warm through. When it is at the point of simmering, dish it, and garnish with forcemeat balls and fried sippets of bread.

Time – To simmer 1 minute.

Average cost – exclusive of the cold meat, 1s 4d.

Sufficient for 5 or 6 persons.

Today's cost

Veal fillet remains £3
Other ingredients 60p

Total £3.60

Stewed Venison

1051. INGREDIENTS – A shoulder of venison, a few slices of mutton fat, 2 glasses of port wine, pepper and allspice to taste, 1 pint of weak stock or gravy, ½ teaspoonful of whole pepper, ½ teaspoonful of whole allspice.

Mode – Hang the venison till tender; take out the bone, flatten the meat with a rolling-pin, and place over it a few slices of mutton fat, which have been previously soaked and pepper, roll the meat up, and bind and tie it securely. Put it into a stewpan with the bone and the above proportion of weak stock or gravy, whole allspice, black pepper, and port wine; cover the lid down closely, and simmer, very gently, from 3 ½ to 4 hours. When quite tender, take off the tape, and dish the meat; strain the gravy over it, and send it to table with redcurrant jelly. Unless the joint is very fat, the above is the best mode of cooking it.

Time – 3 ½ to 4 hours

Average cost – 1s 4d to 1s 6d per lb

Sufficient for 10 or 12 persons

Seasonable – Buck venison, from June to Michaelmas; doe venison, from November to the end of January.

Today's cost

Venison £5
Port £1
Stock 20p

Total £6.20

Baked Tomatoes

(Excellent)

1158. INGREDIENTS – 8 or 10 tomatoes, pepper and salt to taste, 2 oz of butter, bread crumbs.

Mode – Take off the stalks from the tomatoes; cut them into thick slices, and put them into a deep baking-dish; add a plentiful seasoning of pepper and salt, and butter in the above proportion; cover the whole with bread crumbs; drop over these a little clarified butter; bake in a moderate oven from 20 minutes to ½ hour, and serve very hot. This vegetable, dressed as above, is an exceedingly nice accompaniment to all kinds of roast meat. The tomatoes, instead of being cut in slices, may be baked whole; but they will take rather longer time to cook.

Time – 20 minutes to ½ hour.

Average cost, in full season, 9d per basket.

Sufficient for 5 or 6 persons.

Today's Cost £1.75

Another Good Short Crust

1211. INGREDIENTS – To every 1b of flour allow 8 oz. of butter, the yolks of 2 eggs, 2 oz of sifted sugar, about ¼ pint of milk.

Mode – Rub the butter into the flour, add the sugar, and mix the whole as lightly as possible to a smooth paste, with the yolks of eggs well beaten, and the milk. The proportion of the latter ingredient must be judged of by the size of the eggs: if these are large, so much will not be required, and more if the eggs are smaller.

Average cost, 1s per lb.
Today's cost £1 per lb.

Baked Apple Pudding

(Very Good).

1231. INGREDIENTS- 5 moderate-sized apples, 2 tablespoonsfuls of finely-chopped suet, 3 eggs, 3 tablespoonfuls of flour, 1 pint of milk, a little grated nutmeg.

Mode – Mix the flour to a smooth batter with the milk; add the eggs, which should be well whisked, and put this batter into a well-buttered pie-dish. Wipe the apples clean, but do not pare them; cut them in halves, and take out the cores; lay them in the batter, rind uppermost; shake the suet on the top, over which also grate a little nutmeg; bake in a moderate oven for an hour, and cover, when served, with sifted loaf sugar. This pudding is also very good with the applies pared, sliced, and mixed with the batter.

Time – 1 hour. Average cost, 9d

Sufficient for 5 or 6 persons.

Today's cost

Apples £1.20
Flour 50p
Milk 40p
Eggs 50p

Total Cost £2.60

Nesselrode Pudding

(A fashionable iced pudding – Careme's Recipe).

1313. INGREDIENTS – 40 chestnuts, 1 lb of sugar, flavouring of vanilla, 1 pint of cream, the yolks of 12 eggs, 1 glass of Maraschino, 1 oz of candied citron, 2 oz of currants, 2 oz of stoned raisons, ½ pint of whipped cream, 3 eggs.

Mode – Blanch the chestnuts in boiling water, remove the husks, and pound them in a mortar until perfectly smooth, adding a few spoonfuls of syrup. Then rub them through a fine sieve, and mix them in a basin with a pint of syrup made from 1 lb of sugar, clarified, and flavoured with vanilla, 1 pint of cream, and the yolks of 12 eggs. Set this mixture over a slow fire, stirring it without ceasing, and just as it begins to boil, take if off and pass it through a tammy. When it is cold, put it into a freezing-pot, adding the Maraschino, and make the mixture set; then add the sliced citron, the currants, and stoned raisins (these two latter should be soaked the day previously in Maraschino and sugar pounded with vanilla); the whole thus mingled, add a plateful of whipped cream mixed with the whites of 3 eggs, beaten to a froth with a little syrup. When the pudding is perfectly frozen, put it into a pineapple-shaped mould; close the lid, place it again in the freezing-pan, covered over with pounded ice and saltpeter, and let it remain until required for table; then turn the pudding out, and serve.

Time – ½ hour to freeze the mixture.

Seasonable from October to February.

The eager reader will be asking who, what or why is Nesselrode?

Nesselrode pudding was created by French chef Antonie Careme for the Riussian politician, Karl-Robert Vasiliev Nesselrode (1780-1862). We remember nothing of the man's politics but of his sweet tooth - lots for Nesselrode is about the most sugary confection you can concoct. Dentists love it, because it brings them in business.

An Unrivalled Plum-pudding

1326. INGREDIENTS – 1 ½ lb of muscatel raisins, 1 ¾ lb of currants, 1 lb of sultana raisins, 2 lbs of the finest moist sugar, 2 lbs of bread crumbs, 16 eggs, 2 lbs of finely-chopped suet, 6 oz of mixed candied peel, the rind of 2 lemons, 1 oz of ground nutmeg, 1 oz of ground cinnamon, ½ oz of pounded bitter almonds, ¼ pint brandy.

Mode – Stone and cut up the raisins, but do not chop them; wash and dry the currants, and cut the candied peel into thin slices. Mix all the dry ingredients well together, and moisten with the eggs, which should be well beaten and strained, to the pudding; stir in the brandy, and, when all is thoroughly mixed, well butter and flour a stout new pudding-cloth, boil from 6 to 8 hours, and serve with brandy-sauce. A few sweet almonds, blanched and cut in strips, and stuck on the pudding, ornament it prettily. This quantity may be divided and boiled in buttered moulds. For small families this is the most desirable way, as the above will be found to make a pudding of rather large dimensions.

Time – 6 to 8 hours. Average cost, 7s. 6d.

Seasonable in winter. Sufficient for 12 or 14 persons.

Christmas Plum-pudding

(Very Good)

1328. INGREDIENTS- 1 ½ lb of raisins, ½ lb of currants, ½ lb of mixed peel, ¾ lb of bread crumbs, ¾ lb of suet, 8 eggs, 1 wineglassful of brandy.

Mode – Stone and cut the raisins in halves, but do not chop them; wash, pick and dry the currants, and mince the suet finely; cut the candied peel into thin slices, and grate down the bread into fine crumbs. When all these dry ingredients are prepared, mix them well together; then moisten the mixture with the eggs, which should be well beaten, and the brandy; stir well, that everything may be very thoroughly blended, and press the pudding into a buttered mould ite it down tightly with a floured cloth, and boil for 5 or 6 hours. It may be boiled in a cloth without a mould, and will require the same time allowed for cooking. As Christmas puddings are usually made a few days before they are required for table, when the pudding is taken out of the pot, hang it up immediately, and put a plate or saucer underneath to catch the water that may drain from it. The day it is to be eaten, plunge it into boiling water, and keep it boiling for at least 2 hours; then turn it out of the mould, and serve with brandy-sauce. On Christmas-day a sprig of holly is usually placed in the middle of the pudding, and about a wineglassful of brandy poured round it, which, at the moment of serving, is lighted, and the pudding thus brought to table encircled in flame.

Time – 5 or 6 hours the first time of boiling; 2 hours the day it is to be served.

Average cost, 4s.

Sufficient for a quart mould for 7 or 8 persons.

Seasonable on the 25th of December, and on various festive occasions till March.

143

Lemon Creams

(Very good)

1445. INGREDIENTS – 1 pint of cream, 2 dozen sweet almonds, 3 glasses of sherry, the rind and juice of 2 lemons, sugar to taste.

Mode – Blanch and chop the almonds, and put them into a jug with the cream; in another jug put the sherry, lemon-rind, strained juice, and sufficient pounded sugar to sweeten the whole nicely. Pour rapidly from one jug to the other till the mixture is well frothed; then pour it into jelly-glasses, omitting the lemon-rind. This is a very cool and delicious sweet for summer, and may be made less rich by omitting the almonds and substituting orange or raisin wine for the sherry.

Time – Altogether, ½ hour.

Average cost, with cream at 1s per pint, 3s.

Sufficient to fill 12 glasses. Seasonable at any time.

Pineapple Fritters

(An elegant Dish).

1472. INGREDIENTS – A small pineapple, a small wineglassful of brandy or liqueur, 2oz of sifted sugar; batter as for apple fritters No. 1393.

Mode – This elegant dish, although it may appear extravagant, is really not so if made when pineapples are plentiful. We receive them now in such large quantities from the West Indies, that at times they may be purchased at an exceedingly low rate; it would not, of course, be economical to use the pines which are grown in our English pineries for the purposes of fritters. Pare the pine with as little waste as possible, cut it into rather thin slices, and soak these slices in the above proportion of brandy or liqueur and pounded with sugar for 4 hours; then make a batter the same as for apple fritters, substituting cream for the milk, and using a smaller quantity of flour; and, when this is ready, dip in the pieces of pine, and fry them in boiling lard from 5 to 8 minutes; turn them when sufficiently brown on one side, and, when done, drain them from the lard before the fire, dish them on a white d'oyley, strew over them sifted sugar, and serve quickly.

Time – 5 to 8 minutes.

Average cost, when cheap and plentiful, 1s 6d for the pine.

Sufficient for 3 or 4 persons. Seasonable in July and August.

Rice Snowballs

(A pretty dish for Juvenile Suppers)

1479. INGREDIENTS – 6 oz of rice, 1 quart of milk, flavouring of essence of almonds, sugar to taste, 1 pint of custard.

Mode- Boil the rice in the milk, with sugar and a flavouring essence of almonds, until the former is tender, adding, if necessary, a little more milk, should it dry away too much. When the rice is quite soft, put it into teacups, or small round jars, and let it remain until cold ; then turn the rice out on a deep glass dish, pour over custard, and, on the top of each ball place a small piece of bright-coloured preserve or jelly. Lemon-peel or vanilla may be boiled with the rice instead of the essence of almonds when either of these is preferred; but the flavouring of the custard must correspond with that of the rice.

Time – About ¾ hour to swell the rice in the milk.

Average cost, with the custard, 1s 6d.

Sufficient for 5 or 6 children. Seasonable at any time.

Compote of Apricots

(An elegant Dish).

1521. INGREDIENTS- ½ pint of syrup No. 1512, 12 green apricots.

Mode- Make the syrup by recipe No. 1512, and when it is ready, put in the apricots whilst the syrup is boiling. Simmer them very gently until tender, taking care not to let them break; take them out carefully, arrange them on a glass dish, let the syrup cool a little, pour it over the apricots, and, when cold, serve.

Time – From 15-20 minutes to simmer the apricots.

Average cost, 9d.

Sufficient for 4 or 5 persons.
Seasonable in June and July, with green apricots.

To Preserve Cherries in Syrup

(Very delicious)

1529. INGREDIENTS-4 lbs of cherries, 3 lbs of sugar, 1 pint of white-currant juice.

Mode – Let the cherries be as clear and as transparent as possible, and perfectly ripe; pick off the stalks, and remove the stones, damaging the fruit as little as you can. Make a syrup with the above proportion of sugar, by recipe No. 1512; mix the cherries with it, and boil them for about 15 minutes, carefully skimming them; turn them gently into a pan, and let them remain till the next day; then drain the cherries on a sieve, and put the syrup and white-currant juice into the preserving-pan again. Boil these together until the syrup is somewhat reduced and rather thick; then put in the cherries, and let them boil for about 5 minutes; take them off the fire, skim the syrup, put the cherries into small pots or wide-mouthed bottles; pour the syrup over, and when quite cold, tie them down carefully, so that the air is quite excluded.

Time- 15 minutes to boil the cherries in the syrup; 10 minutes to boil the syrup and currant-juice; 5 minutes to boil the cherries the second time.

Average cost for this quantity, 3s, 6d.

Seasonable – Make this in July or August.

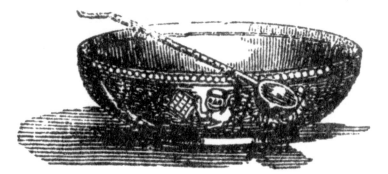

Brillat Savarin's fondue

an excellent recipe

1644 INGREDIENTS - eggs, cheese, butter, pepper and salt

Mode - Take the same number of eggs as there are guests; weigh the eggs in the shell, allow a third of their weight in Gruyere cheese and a piece of butter one sixth of the weight of the cheese. Break the eggs into a basin, beat them well , add the cheese which should be grated and the butter, which should be broken into small pieces. Stir these ingredients together with a wooden spoon, pout the mixture in a lined saucepan, place over the fire and stir until the substance.

Average cost in Mrs Beeton's day 4 shillings.

Today's cost
Eggs £1.00
Butter £1.00
Cheese £2.00
Total £4

A nice useful cake

1757 INGREDIENTS - ¼ lbs of butter, 6oz of currants, ¼ sugar. 1 lb of dried flour, 2 teaspoonfuls of baking powder. 3 eggs, 1 teacup ful of milk, 2oz sweet almonds, 1 oz of candied peel.

Mode – Beat the butter to a cream, wash, pick and dry the currants; whisk the eggs; blanch and chop the almonds and cut the peel into neat slices. When all these are ready, mix the dry ingredients together; then add the butter, milk and eggs and beat the mixture well for a few minutes. Put the cake into a buttered mould or tin and bake it for rather more than 1 ½ hours. The currents and candied peel may be omitted and a little lemon or almond flavouring substituted for them; made in this manner the cake will be found very good.

Time – rather more than 1 ½ hours.

Average cost 1s 9p

Average cost today £1.10

Sunderland Gingerbread nuts

An excellent recipe

1761 INGREDIENTS - 1 ¾ lbs treacle, 1 lb of moist sugar, 1 lb of butter, 2 ¾ lbs flour, 1 ½ oz ground ginger, 1 ½ oz of allspice, 1½ oz of coriander seeds.

Mode – Let the allspice, coriander seeds and ginger be freshly ground put them into a basin with the flour and sugar, and mix these ingredients well together; warm the treacle and the butter together; then with a spoon work into the flour until the whole forms a nice smooth paste. Drop the mixture from the spoon on to a piece of buttered paper and bake in a rather slow oven from 20 minutes to ½ hour. A little candied lemon peel mixed with the above is an improvement and a great authority in culinary matters suggests the addition of a little cayenne pepper in gingerbread. Whether it is advisable to use the latter ingredient or not, we leave to our readers to decide.

Time 20 minutes to ½ hour

Average cost 1s to 1s 4d per lb

Today's cost

Butter £1.20
Flour 75p
Sugar 50p
Total £2.45

A very good seed cake

1776 INGREDIENTS - 1lb butter, 6 eggs, ¾ lbs of sifted sugar, pounded mace and grated nutmeg to taste, 1lb of flour , ¾ oz of caraway seeds, I wineglassful of brandy.

Mode - Beat the butter to a cream; dredge in the flour; add the sugar, mace, nutmeg and caraway seeds and mix these ingredients well in together. Whisk the eggs, stir them with brandy and beat the cake again for 10 minutes. Put into a tin lined with buttered paper and bake it from 1 ½ hours to 2 hours. This cake would be equally nice made with currants.

After this recipe Isabella added a note on bread making in Spain, though I cannot quite track down the train of thought that led to this.

Baking as an Olympic sport

"The bread in the south of Spain is delicious; it is white as snow, close as cake and yet very light; the flavour is most admirable because the wheat is good and pure and bread well kneaded."

And the bakers brought bread forth not just by the sweat of their brow. Isabella added;

"They knead the bread with such force in Spain that the palm of the hand and the second joints of the fingers of the bakers are covered with corns – and it so affects the chest that they cannot work more than two hours at a time."

Gooseberry Vinegar

an excellent recipe

1820 - INGREDIENTS - 2 pecks crystal gooseberries, 6 gallons of water, 12 lbs of foots sugar of the coarsest quality.

Mode – mash the gooseberries (which should be quite ripe) in a tub with a mallet; out them in the water nearly milk warm; let this stand 24 hours; then strain it through a sieve and put the sugar to it, mix it well, then tun it. These proportions are for a 9 gallon cask; and if it be not quite full, more water must be added. Let the mixture be stirred from the bottom of the cask daily for two or three times daily for three or four days to assist in the melting of the sugar; then paste a piece of linen cloth over the bunghole and set the cask in a warm place but not in the sun; any corner of a warm kitchen is the best situation for it. The following spring it should be drawn off into stone bottles and the vinegar will be fit for us twelve months after it is made. This will be found to be a most excellent preparation greatly superior to much that is sold under the name of the best white wine vinegar. Many years experience has proved that pickle made with this vinegar will keep when bought vinegar will not preserve the ingredients. The cost per gallon is merely nominal, especially to those who reside in the country and grow their own gooseberries; the coarse sugar is then the only ingredient to be purchased.

Time – to remain in the cask 9 months.

Average cost - when the gooseberries have to be purchased 1s per gallon, when the gooseberries are grown at home 6d per gallon.

Today's cost
Gooseberries £3 per gallon
Sugar £3
Total cost £6

a very simple and easy method of making a very superior orange wine

1827 INGREDIENTS - 90 Seville oranges, 32 lbs of lump sugar, water.

Mode - Break up the sugar into small pieces and put in a dry sweet 9 gallon cask, placed in a cellar or other storehouse where it is intended to be kept. Have ready close to the cask two large pans or wooden keelers; into one of which put the peel of the oranges pared quite thin and into the other the juice after it has been squeezed from them. Strain the juice through a piece of double muslin and out into the cask with the sugar. Then pour about 1 ½ gallons of water on both the pulp and peels; let it stand for 24 hours and then strain it into the cask. Add more water to the peel and pulp when this has been done and repeat the process every day for a week. It should take about a week to fill up the cask. Be careful to apportion the quantity as nearly as possible to the 7 days and to stir the contents of the cask each day. On the third day after the cask is full - that is the tenth day after the commencement of making – the cask may be securely bunged down. This is a very simple and easy method and the wine made according to it will be pronounced to be most excellent. There is no troublesome boiling and the fermentation takes place in the cask.

When the above directions are attended to, the wine cannot fail to be good. It should be bottled in 8 or 9 months and will be fit for use in a twelvemonth after the time of making. Ginger wine may be made in precisely the same way, only with the 9 gallon cask for ginger wine, 2 lbs of the best whole ginger, bruised, must be put in with the sugar. It will be found convenient to tie the ginger in loosely in a muslin bag.

Time – altogether allow 10 days for the making.

Seasonable make this in March and bottle it the following January.

Average cost 2s 6d per gallon

Today's cost;
32 lbs of sugar £10
90 Seville oranges £15
Total £25

Digesting it all

I never expected to write this book and it seems to me it needs a little Post Script.

The most striking thing I have learned is that in Beeton's day cooking was not just a labour of love but a labour of time. Very few things could be done that fast in the Victorian kitchen and nothing could be done instantly. The only men who cooked – apart from a few eccentrics – were professional chefs. A wife who did not know how to run a kitchen was a pretty poor wife in the eyes of 'Society.'

What is also striking is how the dishes she recommended were essentially British and French. Though the British Empire covered all the globe, there was little interest in multi cultural cooking. There are no Indian or Chinese recipes.

The kebab was never in her mind. And despite her passion for stuffing her text with allusions to ancient Greece, she did not provide one Greek recipe.

Nevertheless some of the themes Beeton insisted on time and time again – that basic ingredients should be fresh and wholesome, that food should be nutritious – are as good advice now as they were then.

I hope too that having digested the book, readers will have some sense of how our everyday domestic lives involve less drudgery. Isabella Beeton did not just write a wonderful book, but one which catches an age, and reading it makes it very plain how much our lives have changed.